The Lemonheads

Editor: **Mike Evans**
Assistant Editor: **Michelle Pickering**
Production Controller: **Michelle Thomas**
Picture Research: **Emily Hedges**
Art Editor: **Ashley Western**
Design: **Design Revolution**

First published in 1994 by
Hamlyn, an imprint of
Reed Consumer Books Limited,
Michelin House, 81 Fulham Road,
London SW3 6RB
and Auckland, Melbourne, Singapore and Toronto

A Catalogue record for this book is available from the British Library
ISBN 0–600–58425–9

Printed in Spain by Cayfosa, Barcelona

Picture Acknowledgements

Dan Estabrook: 41, 50 top, 51 top;

Jill Furmanovsky: 73, 75, 79;

Liane Hentscher: 71 background, 78 centre;

London Features International: 7, 58 top right Derek Ridgers: 54, 55;

Melody Maker: 4, 29 bottom Ellen Comskey: 59 bottom Joe Dilworth: 45 Steve
Gullick: 11, 62, 63 right, 64 Liane Hentscher: 9 top left, 42 centre Michael Levine:
5, 6, 9 bottom right Mike Morton: 40 top left, 41 below centre Phil Nicholls: 21,
30 Jesse Peretz: 61 Pat Pope: 8 top right and bottom left Alan Rewell: 24 top
right Tom Sheehan: 20 bottom, 24 bottom right Stephen Sweet: 32, 40 bottom
right, 42 top and bottom, 44 bottom left, 48, 49 top right, 52 top, 68, 77 bottom
left Taang!: 37 Taang!/Todd Ensley: 33 Taang!/Dan Estabrook: 39
Taang!/Stephanie Hoffman: 38 Kevin Westenberg: 20 top;

Jesse Peretz: 14, 18-19, 26, 27 top, centre and bottom, 28, 29 top, 35, 43, 49 bottom, 52 bottom, 53, 57 top, centre and bottom, 58 left, 60, 65 top centre and bottom, 67, 71 inset, 72 inset, 76, 77 top;

Redferns: Susan Moore: 50 bottom, 51 bottom Ebet Roberts: 46, 80;

Relay: Dave Wainwright: 78 left and right;

Retna: Lindsay Brice: 7 Steve Double: 65 bottom left Steve Gullick: 66 top right
Neal Preston: 69 Steve Rapport: 3 Ed Sirrs: 59 top;

S.I.N: 47 David Anderson: 10 Liane Hentscher: 44 top right, 49 top left, 52 centre,
56 left, centre and right Tony Mott: 15 background Paul Stanley: 12;

Brooke Williams: 13, 16, 17, 22, 23, 24 left, 25, 34, 63 left, 72 background

The Lemonheads

E V E R E T T   T R U E

HAMLYN

CONTENTS

Big Gay Heart

I was born in the Summer Of Love and I've come to say 'Hi!' – Evan Dando. I first met Lemonheads singer Evan Dando in a hotel lobby in Stuttgart, Germany, in the spring of '91.

At the time, Dando was indistinguishable from any of his fellow Bostonian musicians: warm, home-fed good looks, half-attempted fringe flopping around in front of his face, baggy sweater and checked shirt. He'd probably taken a few drugs – but that was okay, everyone else had. When he spoke, it was with a slightly misleading lazy drawl. His own press agent didn't even recognise him when we first walked into the building.

Checking in at the desk, the PR pronounced firmly: 'Right. Now we should find the band.'

I pointed to where three, clearly American boys were standing, five feet away from us: 'Isn't that Evan over there?'

Sure, it was Evan with fellow Lemonheads Jesse Peretz (aka Jesse Pool Jesse) and David Ryan, come to rock the shores of Germany once more, set them aglow with their own passionate take on East Coast US collegiate rock (chunky guitars, hearts worn well-high on sleeves, gently wry lyrics).

The singer ambled over and made his introductions.

We discovered we had a friend in common: Daniel Treacy of sometimes wacky, sometimes heart-rending UK psychedelic popsters, Television Personalities. He wasn't the only interest we shared, however.

We both loved the Pixies; we both dug Big Star and the tragic country rocker Gram Parsons. That much was apparent, just from the slight country twang which has always resonated inside Lemonheads songs. The crucial incisiveness and fury of Neil Young, the dark side of warped, all-American heroes The Beach Boys, Howe Gelb's ramshackle, pungent Giant Sand, the guitar pyrotechnics of J Mascis's incendiary Dinosaur Jr, author James Joyce's abstract insightfulness . . . yeah, we had plenty to talk about. Evan's always held a torch for the loser, the unsung romantic.

Tales were told: of a New Year's Eve show the year the Berlin Wall came tumbling down, with glasses held high and guitars strummed chaotically; of long, leafy, winding New England lanes and parched, porched

The Lemonheads – Nic Dalton, David Ryan, Evan Dando, 1993

houses which looked as if they'd been lifted straight from *The Shining*; of a spanking new pop trio from Boston called Blake Babies, and their singer, the icy-cool, virginal Juliana Hatfield; of splits and spats and female tour managers who punch out singers' girlfriends when they become too much to bear; of alcohol abstinence, angst and alleyways; of loves, lives and famous authors' takes on same.

I believe it was Milan Kundera, author of *The Unbearable Lightness Of Being*, who wrote: 'When in love, the sight of the beloved has a completeness that no words and no embrace can match, a completeness which only the act of making love can temporarily accommodate.' Whatever.

It was a quote I threw at Evan at our very first meeting.

It struck me then that what The Lemonheads were attempting to approximate through their spirited, harmony-led, three-chord thrash was a non-verbal understanding of that self-same completeness. A trifle pretentious, perhaps – but all their songs seemed to lead to one thing: trying to capture *the moment*.

Evan, wisely, demurred from answering the charge directly – 'They're just confusion songs,' he laughed.

Evan and Juliana Hatfield, Reading, '93

Evan Dando wanders unnoticed through the crowd at the 1993 Reading festival

JUST THREE SHORT YEARS AGO

The Lemonheads came across as three affable, intelligent, easy-going boys. All qualities you'd expect from a band who treated music more as a hobby than a profession (indeed, Evan had quit The Lemonheads several times); all qualities you'd expect from anyone who'd grown up within spitting distance of the dreaming spires of Harvard University, home of all things powerful and American.

Difficult to interview, perhaps – but only cos they were more interested in talking about anything but themselves.

'I like it because it has this proud sparrow feel – the sparrow puffing out its chest,' Evan explained when I asked him about The Lemonheads' then-current single, a cover of Trini Lopez's 'Gonna Get Along Without You Now'.

'It's very punk, actually.'

Evan grew up as a well-educated high school kid who probably could have gone on to become a successful attorney (like his father) or, at the very least, a catalogue clothes model. But he had a voice – and a very expressive, mournful voice it was too.

Dando in action

And it was far more suited to the intricacies of a Trini Lopez song ('Just a promotional item to help the tour,' as the singer coyly put it) than The Lemonheads' earlier Husker Du-saturated offerings.

Bassist Jesse, meanwhile, was a film-school student. He later dropped out of The Lemonheads to concentrate full-time on his filmmaking and has since shot several Lemonheads sleeves and videos, including 1993's 45-minute-long tour memento, 'Two Weeks In Australia'. Drummer David Ryan was (famously) a former pastry baker who first met Evan when the singer used to come into his shop after late-night sessions playing bass with Blake Babies.

We hung out by the canal and railway tracks at the side of the cavernous venue – originally built as a C&W club for American GIs stationed in Germany – kicked stones, exchanged American and British jokes, and generally attempted to fill up some of the ever-present tedium of touring. Evan showed me how to whistle two notes simultaneously; I showed him how to warble like a thrush. The journalist and the band swapped phone numbers – just in case any of us happened to be passing through each other's towns.

It was just another day on the Continental treadmill, no different and no less fun than the thousand that had preceded it and the thousand that were to follow.

The show that night was typically chaotic: noise and melodies wailing back from Evan's guitar in equal proportions as he shook his hair and generally attempted to appear the toughest, roughest, meanest, mummy's boy rocker on the block. Suzanne Vega's 'Luka' was decimated in a blurred squall of fractured drumming; old favourites 'Mallo Cup' and 'Hate Your Friends' blistered where they fell.

The reaction from the crowd was suitably histrionic.

That was The Lemonheads then, back in March 1991. Just another (slightly superior) Boston college rock band on the make; another cool, punky East Coast outfit seemingly doomed to spend a lifetime playing to its own passionate cult following.

But The Lemonheads had three crucial differences – the songs, the voice and the looks.

All this, just three short years ago.

DIPPY DANDO

I last met Evan Dando backstage at a Lemonheads/Hole concert in LA at the end of 1993.

In the interim, his face has been plastered across countless front covers, posters, gossip columns. His band have had songs featured in *Wayne's World 2* and chosen to help promote the video of *The Graduate*. His name has been linked with Kylie Minogue, Madonna, Juliana Hatfield. You'd have to be media-illiterate not to recognise him now.

He greets me with his trademark, indifferent yet somehow sincere hug which could have – and probably has been – given to any one of 10,000 industry people. The singer has gained somewhat of a reputation as an airhead over the past year, which has

probably come about partly as a result of his willingness to 'grip and grin', to 'press the flesh', to greet everyone around him like they are his long-lost drug buddies – whether he's met them before, or not.

His manager informs him that I think his latest album (the band's sixth), 'Come On Feel The Lemonheads', is my favourite album of 1993.

He shrugs. Must have been told the same thing a dozen times by a dozen different starfuckers. He must be fed up to the back teeth with 'Yes' people. He must long for the simple pleasures of mid-Eighties Boston sometimes.

The album – a sometimes cynical, sometimes tearingly honest take on his current lifestyle – has soundtracked

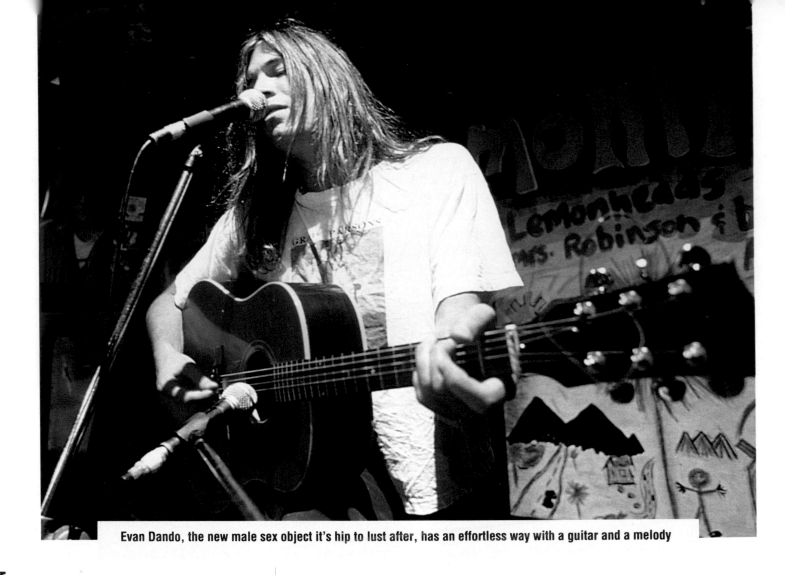

Evan Dando, the new male sex object it's hip to lust after, has an effortless way with a guitar and a melody

numerous journeys I've made. I empathise with most of its concerns and yet I've never felt further away from Evan Dando.

We exchange pleasant small talk, and I think of all those names people have called him: Dippy Dando, Evan the Human Dildo, a Himbo, Slacker-Jawed.

I watch Evan as he chuckles and bumbles in his endearing way, and I think to myself that perhaps the singer dropped one too many tabs of E once too often during his stays in Australia (the place where he wrote most of 'Come On Feel The Lemonheads' with current songwriting partner Tom Morgan).

I think perhaps he's a just little too publicly airheaded for his own good, and that he knows it too. And that maybe he doesn't care, realising that the less threatening you appear to be, the more people will let you get away with.

I know he's smart, he knows he's smart, but he sure gives a great impersonation of someone who's several bound volumes short of a library.

Hanging backstage with Hole before the show, there's a knock on the door and two 'Evan groupies' poke their freckled faces shyly into the room. Neither of them can be older than 13. Courtney Love, the waif-like, bedraggled wife of late-Nirvana singer Kurt Cobain, queries them closely as to quite how far they've 'been' with Evan. Although one of them was involved in an infamous incident with the singer on a trans-Atlantic flight, you'll be relieved to hear (I'm sure) that nothing illegal transpired between them.

With his matinee idol looks and tousled skate-punk style, the singer has quickly gained a reputation as both a first-class flirt and slut. He's become the new male sex object it's hip to lust after.

Christina Kelly, editor of cool US teenage girls' magazine *Sassy*, has been known to swoon whenever his name is mentioned. Kylie Minogue was meant to have been spotted canoodling with him down under. *Spin* magazine had him engaged in an icky tongue sandwich with some supermodel or other for a

front cover. Longtime friend Juliana Hatfield – another in the new generation of guitar hero pin-ups for the 'alternative' kids – constantly has her name linked to his, despite continued protestations from both sides that they are merely friends.

Even Madonna was rumoured to have rung him up for a date.

(This was later revealed as a particularly mean joke played on Evan by Nirvana and producer Steve Albini. The Seattle band were fooling around in the studio one day while recording 'In Utero' and phoned Evan in LA, pretending to be Madonna's personal manager. They kept Evan hanging on for ages. The singer remains unrepentant. 'If Madonna called me, I'd *still* jerk off,' he told *Rolling Stone* magazine.)

I watch Evan fooling around, making some hot moves on a stray skateboard, sound-checking down the mic with an *a cappella* version of 'Being Around', and find myself increasingly unable to separate fact from fiction, illusion from reality.

A GREAT, GREAT BAND

1993 has been quite a tempestuous year for Mr Dando. The release of the much underrated 'Come On Feel The Lemonheads' was far overshadowed by both his status as the Number One male heartthrob for the grunge generation and his continued determination to be the living embodiment of the phrase 'sex, drugs and rock 'n' roll' – with the emphasis on the DRUGS.

One notorious interview Evan gave to the music press at the height of his extended lost weekend in Los Angeles, just as he was finishing up the final mixes of 'Come On Feel The Lemonheads' in August '93, had the star answering questions with the help of a note pad – he had lost his voice through smoking too much crack cocaine.

Spookily, that 'lost weekend' began when he played the first night of friend Johnny Depp's Viper Rooms – the same venue that River Phoenix was to be found dead outside a few months later in true *Hollywood Babylon*-style circumstances.

Indeed, a while back, a bunch of music critics made Evan odds-on to be the first of the new grunge superstars to OD, thus emulating his hero Gram Parsons.

So I stare at Evan and I wonder: is Mr Lemonhead just another college rocker who got lucky, the 'new Elvis Costello', a lightweight fraud, a much vilified genius, a fanciful object of desire, a fucked-up airhead, or none of these things? And what does it matter, just as long as the music's good?

Because if Evan really is as lazy, as dumb, as brain-addled as his critics say, then how come he can write songs as great as 'Stove', 'Sad Girl', 'Bit Part', 'Style' – indeed, the whole of 'Come On Feel The Lemonheads', an album which is shot through with a peculiar tenderness, melancholy and wry understanding of the dirty business he's involved in?

How is it that Evan can write a song as moving as 'Big Gay Heart', an anti gay-bashing song, whose title was inspired by Johnny Depp after the actor described his own pad as a 'big gay place'. People have described his songs as throwaway, but perhaps they're confusing the image with the content. How is it that Evan can write and sing 'Style' – the consummate 'Should I get fucked up now?' number – with such grace? It's a song which is both inch-perfect in its execution and choice of guest star to sing back-up on it (funkateer Rick James).

How is it that he can write songs which appear so 'surface' on a cursory listen, yet which resonate round in my head long after other 'weightier' songs have disappeared? Even 'Being Around' – the song which contains the infamous lines 'If I were a booger/Would you blow your nose?' – even that childlike list of abstract observations contains more simple heady truths than any number of fancy words and phrases.

Perhaps what the critics find so damning about Evan Dando is best explained by the lines I wrote in February 1993 in the introduction to my *Melody Maker* cover story on The Lemonheads.

Always ready to oblige: Evan poses for the cameras in true idol fashion, January '93

'Don'tcha just hate people like Evan Dando?' I asked back then. 'He's cool, good-looking, non-judgmental, lovable, with never an unkind word to say about anyone. He's warm, affectionate, a pin-up to a generation of hipster teenage girls, has an effortless way with a guitar and a melody, and holidays in Australia for half the year.

'He hangs out with filmstars, hails from an affluent background, has been called the new Costello, is friendly and self-assured. His band is talked about in *Smash Hits* and *Melody Maker* with equal respect. He's intelligent, sussed and blessed with the looks of a bleached surfer god, or maybe a windswept skateboard king. The list goes on . . . '

How dare he be so good-looking AND have the voice to match? A voice so effortlessly evocative that it stunned a hardened crowd of UK industry cynics when it performed solo, with just an acoustic for company, at Ronnie Scott's the previous Christmas. The show went into extra time and beyond, as the crowd refused to let him go.

How dare he have a voice that can drape new layers of meaning into the doomed torch classic 'Gloomy Tuesday', a voice that can sound fuckable and huggable and wistful all at once? How dare he possess a voice that can – seemingly without any effort on its user's part at all – transform a camp hippy number such as 'Frank Mills' (from the soundtrack to *Hair*) into a yearning torch song, one which seems to sum up all the hopes and despairs and tender brutalness of chance meetings in under two-and-a-half minutes?

At the show in LA, I look at Evan, flicking his hair back from his eyes in front of a crowd mostly comprised of frankly delirious, gusset-dampened teen girls, and I'm damned if I can work out where the illusion begins or where the illusion ends any more, he plays the part so well.

And you know something?

It doesn't matter in the slightest. Cos The Lemonheads are a great, great band.

Courting controversy in dress and pigtails at Reading festival, 1993

Early Days

Even as a child, Evan Dando was the most popular boy in his class, the one the girls would all lust after. The cool, laidback, hippy-esque kid. The one with the looks *and* the intelligence, skateboard and S-levels. The one who'd take all the lead roles in school plays. As his only sister, Holly Dando, confirmed when I met her in February 1993, chaperoning for Evan during a mini-tour of the UK.

Quite why there was a need for Evan to take a chaperone around with him is another matter: some say to keep him away from the teenage girls; some say to keep him off the Jack Daniels and hard drugs; some say it was cos it's a good excuse to give his elder sister – cool, affable, in real life a hospital worker in NYC – free holidays. I suspect the latter. His mother has accompanied him on other trips. Then again, she's a renowned hipster who still rollerskates in Central Park and goes to indie rock shows on her own.

'When people ask me if I find it weird that my brother is becoming famous, some kind of rock god,' Holly stated, 'I tell them he's always been like that – he's always been a rock god. Even in kindergarten, all the girls were in love with him. People would come running up to me and go, "Are you *Evan's* sister?" He was always special.'

Evan was going steady with a girl called Anna-Lee Hill in kindergarten by the age of four. They'd stand by the swings, hold hands and stare longingly into each other's eyes.

His first kiss came at the age of eight: 'I was staying over at my friend Freddie Dearborn's house,' he told UK teenage girls' magazine *Just 17*. 'His sister was a hot sixth-grade babe who took a shine to me. I put my head on her shoulder while we were watching telly. Later, we all went for a walk up this mountain and just started making out. I remember, we even charged Freddie a dollar to watch us!'

SUMMER OF LOVE CHILD

Holly and Evan grew up in an area slightly to the north of Boston, in the rural suburb of Essex, Massachusetts – a real Yankee environment. Possessions were slightly frowned upon (Evan was, after all, a Summer Of Love child, born 4/3/67, 'conceived on a house boat in Sausalito'), so the family always dressed down slightly, cautious not to waste anything. Imagine the home of an artistic, tuned-in fashion model married to a hip real estate attorney with shoulder-length hair. Rumours of the Dando family's vast fortune (once estimated at $6 million) are greatly exaggerated, however.

'We always hung out with a lot of rich people,' Evan demurred, while explaining his own family were comfortably middle-class.

Reports of his early childhood sound idyllic – forever bunking off on surfing expeditions or being invited to girls' birthday parties where our man Dando would be the only boy present. The Dandos – father Jeffrey, mother Susan, Holly and Evan – lived in Essex until Evan was nine, when they moved to Boston's North Shore.

'I remember my parents during the mid-Seventies as these real hippy groovers,' Evan told *Just 17*. 'They partied regularly, and they liked surfing. So every other summer we'd go to Berlitz in Canada to surf. They were always dragging my sister and me around in search of *that* perfect wave.'

'As kids, we had everything we really wanted,' Holly recalled. 'We had cool vacations, a nice house, went to private school, but my parents were very careful not to make us too conscious of it. You know, like when you're a kid you ask your

The Dandos: Evan, Jeffrey, Holly, Susan

parents if you're rich or if you're poor. They'd always tell us it didn't matter.'

When Evan was about 11, his parents split up – an event that still affects the singer deeply. From being a sunny, carefree kid, Evan became increasingly moody, sitting alone in his room for hours on end, strumming an acoustic guitar. He was later to write about the experience in the song 'Confetti'.

'That song is about the way people go along with a relationship without really caring about it, just to keep the other person happy,' he told me. 'It's about laziness.'

'It was bad,' he says now, referring to the split. 'I felt abandoned. I stayed with my mum and sister, but while *they* talked about it, I was considered a little boy who wouldn't understand such things. Meanwhile, my dad went off with this woman who was into, like, *macramé . . .*

'I mean, she was perfectly nice,' he told *Maker*'s Sally Margaret Joy, 'but, um, my parents were like the perfect couple. They were even in commercials on television. The thing was, *inside* he wasn't going along with it. And so he just snapped, he just took off. I was alone, at the age of 11 or 12, and that just confused me even more. And I guess abandonment always produces some sort of anger. I formed a punk band and that helped a lot, to bash it out.

'When my parents divorced,' he continues, 'I didn't really register how much it bothered me at the time. It came up in other ways. I was an angry kid. In my teens, I was a bit of a vandal and quite destructive.

I've mellowed out since then, become a lot happier. I've come to terms with my anger.'

It's strange. Looking at the image of Evan Dando on countless billboards and front covers, you wouldn't have thought he was the type to have suffered any major traumas or mood-swings.

Listening to the music, however – from the early temper tantrums of 'I Don't Wanna' and 'Hate Your Friends' off the debut album, to the melancholy cover versions of Abba songs and Gram Parsons numbers – it makes sense. And knowing his tendency to run away to Australia when the whole business gets too much to bear, it makes perfect sense.

'I do have a tendency to gloss over my past,' he told me good-naturedly. 'In social situations, I'd rather have a good time and laugh. But I've been a bit of a schizoid guy in the past.'

His sister agreed.

'He wasn't the type to influence or manipulate others,' she explained. 'His temperament was the same as it is now, in that you can never depend on Evan's mood. He'll not bend to any external pressure, he'll be exactly how he wants to be, and screw everyone else's needs.'

For a while, Evan went slightly off the rails, becoming (in his own words) a 'teenage delinquent'. He'd drop acid, throw rocks at cars, skateboard and generally misbehave. During free periods in school, he'd go up to the roof of his mother's spacious apartment, 20 storeys up, and, with a few friends, smoke pot until they got high. He eventually moved away when he was 18, to a 'closet in a friend's house'.

Rock music obviously helped shape some of his actions. His sister protectively put this behaviour down to the influence of a 'few bad friends'.

'Evan's had his share of traumas,' Holly says. 'Our parents' divorce was the biggie. It was a very, very wrenching experience for the whole family. Losing his stuffed koala bear on a trip to Barbados – that was another big one! But in the general scheme of life, he's had a very good experience.'

THREE HIGH SCHOOL KIDS

Just a few blocks away from the world-famous *Cheers* bar lies Commonwealth School. Back when Evan was growing up, it had a reputation for being the most liberal and progressive school in town. There were no rules, no dress code. Evan loved the place, spending five years there. (He was to spend a much shorter time at Skidmore College later, dropping out almost immediately after he enrolled.)

'The only rule was that you couldn't rollerskate in class,' his sister laughs. 'Evan had amazing teachers who, in another life, would have been Harvard professors. He was writing papers on Hegelian dialectic and Kafka's diaries in tenth grade – he was three years younger than me and kicking my ass.'

Don't you hate people like that?

'Yeah,' she grimaces, 'but he had a hard time there. He would get an A in composition and an F in math. It was a rocky road. A lot of those kids were so smart and motivated on their own, they could trip all weekend and then come back and do school. Evan wasn't like that. He was always wanting to do the drugs, but he wasn't sure about the schoolwork. He was going through a hard time emotionally because of our parents' divorce, though.'

'People used to call me Mr Popularity at high school,' Evan himself recalled, 'but they were being ironic [he's since contradicted himself on this point]. I was not popular there. At grade school I was a loner too. The loner on the swings, you know?'

It was at Commonwealth High School in the fall of '81 that Evan first met Ben Deily and Jesse Peretz, later to become the original line-up of The Lemonheads.

Jesse – an easy-going kid from a middle-class Cambridge family of six, son of *New Republic* editor-in-chief Marty Peretz – remembers that when they first met, Evan was already 'the really handsome guy who knew it'.

'Evan was the guy who, even in ninth grade, would always sleep with the hottest senior girl,' he says. 'Even back then people hated him cos of that. It could be slightly nauseating, how good-looking his family were. When you saw Evan walking down the street with his mother, he'd look like he was stepping out with this totally gorgeous older chick. All that family were beautiful.

'Evan was definitely the total fuck-up in school from his teachers' standpoint, though,' he confirms. 'But he also had his subjects, like English literature, where he could be incredibly sharp and astute when he set his mind to it. Those subjects were the only reason he didn't get kicked out. He's never been one to edit anything that went through his brain.

'He's never been real good at communicating his feelings in any way, either.' Jesse never heard Evan mention his parents' divorce at school, and it wasn't until some years later that the bassist finally met Evan's father.

'He doesn't know how to sustain heavy friendships,' Jesse explains. 'No more now than in high school, except that nowadays he can't be alone because he always has his entourage around.

'Neither one of us was that into punk,' he continues, 'but we had the same friends. I've always thought he was pretty mean, especially early on, but when he got his hair cut, that became more like punk rock meanness than anything. Often, he'd respond very harshly with some level of accuracy about something that was going on, and I'd wonder why he didn't shut the fuck up. He's not even vaguely that way anymore, however.'

Ben Deily – who was soon to join Evan on his early musical experiments – came from a background which was almost a caricature of a wealthy liberal Cambridge family, with all the attendant 'radicalism' and Political Correctness. (Cambridge is the suburb of Boston nearest to Harvard.)

Ben's mother and stepfather were always appearing in adult theatre group productions and musicals such as Gilbert & Sullivan's *HMS Pinafore* (their van had a sticker on its side which read 'Acting Builds Character'). The Deilys were the type of family who would all wear kimonos when they ate Japanese food.

The three boys soon found they had a common interest in music.

Evan had been interested in music from an early age, according to his sister. This was partly down to his parents' record collection, which included anything from Motown (Martha Reeves, Stevie Wonder) to Steely Dan, Marvin Gaye to Neil Young, the soundtrack of *Hair* to Al Green, Sly Stone to the pre-grunge sound of The Sonics to the sweet country harmonies of The Louvin Brothers. And plenty more besides.

His dad turned him on to Jesse Colin Young; his sister used to play Black Sabbath records to him.

'Evan taught himself to play guitar when he was only 10 years old,' Holly recalls. 'The first thing I remember him writing was a jazz piece for piano, which was played at school assembly. Overnight, Evan went from liking Led Zeppelin to writing full-force jazz to getting into punk bands like Minor Threat [their singer Ian MacKaye now fronts inspirational straight-edge punks, Fugazi].'

'By the age of 10,' says current drummer and long-term friend David Ryan, 'Evan would be standing by the jukebox, staring at it, pumping quarters into it, playing old soul records. He was a musicologist, even then.'

A few years after his parents' divorce, Evan started to lose interest in the simpler pursuits of adolescence.

Instead, after his sister gave him a book (*The Family*) about the hippy serial killer and self-proclaimed messiah Charles Manson, he started to become obsessed with the darker side of Sixties America.

In this, he shares a similar penchant to many of his American musical contemporaries – most American 'underground' bands are fascinated with serial killers of one kind or another. (The Lemonheads covered Manson's winsome love song 'Your Home Is Where You're Happy' on their second album 'Creator', long before any of the Guns N' Roses furore.)

Evan shaved off all his hair – styling it short, blond and spiky – started jamming with Ben Deily and formed a punk band.

The Lemonheads' career had begun.

★★★★★★·★★★★★★★

Hate Your Friends

Pixies And Dinosaurs

It was the final months of 1985. The Replacements and Husker Du were finally starting to break big. Post-hardcore labels such as SST and Homestead were at the height of their dominance of the US underground rock scene. Evan Dando and Ben Deily had been playing together as a duo for some time, mostly covering songs by groups like The Angry Samoans.

The Pixies who, according to legend, headlined the first-ever Lemonheads gig

despite the fact that the last time he'd played rock was as a guitarist in his Junior high school band, The Drainpipes. The initial team-up was meant to be a one-off only: all the musicians had college to worry about later that year – Ben and Jesse were going to Harvard to study English literature, and film and photography, respectively; Evan was away to Skidmore.

(The singer lasted just three months there before he drifted back to Boston to get a job working at a tennis club: 'I lasted one semester,' Evan told *NME*. 'I got one D-minus and four Fs, and spent all my money on drugs. I ended up saying "fuck this" and drove away in a snowstorm.')

The day after they played together, Evan went away on holiday for six weeks. When he returned, he decided he'd enjoyed playing in a proper band and recalled Jesse.

And thus the band that was shortly to become The Whelps and thereafter The Lemonheads started life. According to legend, their debut gig was supporting the then-embryonic Pixies.

Initially, they were a hardcore, three-chord Husker Du/Replacements-type outfit. Songs were thrashy, speedy affairs, augmented by the odd guitar overdub and cover version. Another big influence on the early Lemonheads were local Homestead band, Dinosaur Jr:

'We used to really admire that band's attitude when we started,' Evan told *Melody Maker* in 1992. 'They were so cool, and they

In November 1985, Evan and Ben recorded two of their own songs for posterity on the school four-track as part of a class project. One of these was an early version of 'So I Fucked Up', which was later to resurface on their first EP and album. Inspired by the experience, the duo decided to continue playing together, with a view to recording some more of their tracks in a 'proper' studio the day after they graduated from high school the following summer.

In March 1986 the pair asked Jesse Peretz, then jazz bassist in the school band, if he wanted to play with them. He said yes,

Seminal influence: Dinosaur Jr

didn't take anything too seriously. Dinosaur did a lot for me back in the mid-Eighties. They brought rock back from those bands like Frankie Goes To Hollywood, who I didn't like at all. Dinosaur weren't afraid to relax and play loud, heavy, psychedelic rock. After they came along, I never felt self-conscious about liking Black Sabbath.'

Most of Evan's original compositions, written when the singer was about 15 years old, were the standard 'boy-gets-into-relationship-with-girl-and-wonders-what's-going-on-here-type songs', according to his sister, who was a slightly bemused onlooker by this point.

BIRTH OF A BAND

At this point the band were nameless – and remained so until it came to releasing their first single, 'Laughing All The Way To The Cleaners'. Almost all histories of The Lemonheads up until now have named The Whelps as the band who immediately preceded them. According to Jesse, however, The Whelps never actually existed.

'People totally over-exaggerate The Whelps angle,' he told me. 'We were never officially called that. When we were going to put out our debut single, we had to come up with a name, so we called ourselves The Whelps. But after about 10 days of that, people began telling us that the name "fucking sucks, you fucking loser assholes!" Or something similar. So we began to have second thoughts.

'While I was finishing off the artwork, Ben went away, and Evan and I were convinced by our schoolfriend Ivan to change the name to The Lemonheads. That change was the cause of one our first big wars with Ben, when he came back and discovered we'd changed the sleeve and everything to incorporate the band's new name.'

Ivan got the name from a well-known midwestern sweet – whose packs ironically bear the motto 'Just Say No To Drugs!' (This wasn't the end of Ivan's association with the band: his Andy Warhol-like features were later to grace the front cover of the band's second album, 'Creator'.)

'It seemed to fit,' said Dando about their new name, 'because Lemonheads are sweet on the outside and sour on the inside. It certainly helped the manufacturers shift a few packets!'

And thus The Lemonheads were born.

TOP OF THE COCK

The three boys had played together as a unit once before, however. Commonwealth School had an event called The Hancock

'We played Bob Marley songs,' Jesse recalls, laughing at the memory. 'One particular song we did was called 'Ecumenical Room', which arose out of the fascination with Jewishness at the school, because there were so many Jewish kids there.'

THINGS JUST SEEMED TO HAPPEN

'Why make a record?' asks Jesse now. 'Why not? Someone was playing some songs.' Throughout their early history, The

The four-song seven-inch EP was recorded in just one day, early June 1986.

It contained the band's first version of 'Glad I Don't Know' (later re-recorded for 'Lick'), the adrenaline-driven 'I Like To' and possibly the best song Ben Deily ever wrote, the passionate and surly 'So I Fucked Up'. Evan sang and played guitar on the first two tracks, Ben on the third. This way of playing songs was to stay the norm, right up until the point when Ben left the group.

twice a year where all the students would go up to New Hampshire for three days, where the school's founder had a farm. It happened once in the spring and once in the fall. Each day was composed of random activities and, at night, there was a choice between sleeping up in the dorm, or in the barn with the co-eds. That barn in New Hampshire inevitably ended up as the place where 90 per cent of Commonwealth boys lost their virginity.

In tenth grade, Evan, Jesse and Ben got a band together and practised for the whole three days of The Hancock, performing under the name Top Of The Cock.

Lemonheads were totally unmotivated. Things just seemed to happen. The main reason behind writing songs appeared to be, 'Well, we have to play *something*!' Cover versions were decided upon by what was popular at the time ('Luka') or what the band had just heard on the radio ('I Am A Rabbit').

Someone suggested they should go into a studio to make a single, so they did. A fellow waiter at Rebecca's in Boston (where Jesse was working as a busboy) told the bassist about someone who could record groups cheaply, so the band thought they'd take advantage of the opportunity. Their debut single cost just $200 to make.

The fourth song on the single was the cover version of Proud Scum's 'I Am A Rabbit' (later to appear on CD versions of 'Lick', alongside a third Evan Dando song from the sessions, 'Mad').

Why did The Lemonheads choose to cover a song by an obscure New Zealand punk outfit? Its inclusion came about because of the direct influence of the Harvard University radio station, WHRB. All through May it was the station's habit to broadcast what they called their 'orgy period', where the DJs would examine a genre of music in minutest detail. In 1986, they had their biggest orgy period ever

– a solid week, 168-hour breakdown of punk rock, starting with Sixties punk and going all the way round the world.

All the 'fucking loser geeks from Commonwealth' (as Jesse put it) skipped class to listen. During one of the 10-hour sessions, dedicated to playing punk rock from the Antipodes, a local DJ called Curtis W Casella played the Proud Scum song.

Curtis was an oldtime punk rocker, idolised by all the new punk kids in Boston.

single themselves. Another DJ from the station, Patrick Armory, split the manufacturing costs with the band, and so 1,000 copies of the record came out, half on the band's own label (Huh-Bag) and half on the DJ's (Armory Arms).

The trio helped promote the EP with a couple of live shows at clubs like Boston's Rat Club, and it quickly sold out – a remarkable achievement for a self-distributed record. There again, their poppy take on

Right there and then, he decided to give the band half the money to record what was to become their debut album.

A FINE WAY TO START A CAREER

The first half of 'Hate Your Friends' (originally titled 'Six') was recorded in September on an eight-track, with Jesse Peretz on bass, Evan Dando on guitar and drums, and Ben Deily on guitar and drums. It was recorded mostly live, but with two overdubs of guitar.

A DJ at WHRB despite the fact that he never attended Harvard, he had the biggest record collection in town and wasn't above bootlegging the odd rare single when the occasion arose – or so Jesse claims! He'd set up Taang! records a couple of years before, specifically to release an EP by a Boston skatecore band called Gang Green. The Lemonheads wanted to release their EP on his label, but Curtis – not knowing whether Taang! was a full-time concern or not – turned them down.

He did, however, offer to include 100 copies of the record in a Gang Green mailout, if the band agreed to press up the

punk happened to fit in exactly with what was the in-vogue sound of the moment.

Later that summer, while Evan was away up in New York State attending college and popping down to Costa Rica to experiment with cocaine, Jesse Peretz got his own show at WHRB. He'd spend whole nights up there, just chewing the fat with Curtis and playing old punk records. It was during one of these sessions that he decided to play Curtis the Ben Deily song 'So I Fucked Up'.

Curtis listened to it on the studio's old tape machine, rewound it, listened to it again, rewound it, listened to it – all the time becoming more and more enthusiastic.

For the second half, recorded a few months later in January 1987, the band recruited local drummer Doug Trachton to help out.

Doug only stayed in The Lemonheads for as long as they needed to finish the album, however.

'Doug was one of the most kind-hearted people I've ever met,' Ben Deily told *Record Collector*. 'He was very nice. But, among other things, he had an earring and a mohawk, and at that time Evan and Jesse were into having a restrained appearance. He didn't last long.'

Jesse remembers it slightly differently. 'We had to get rid of this guy Doug pretty

quick,' he informs me, 'because he was a weird freak who kept stealing shit from people. He was totally gross to look at as well – one side of his head was shaved and he had dreadlocks down the back.'

The Lemonheads fired Doug 25 minutes after a show they played at Harvard University, with Bullet Lavolta and Blake Babies as support. Blake Babies drummer John Strohm was immediately enlisted to help out.

'Hate Your Friends' came out in June 1987. On the cover was an old black-and-white photo of Jesse's brother. On the reverse was a shot of the four-piece band (with Doug) which included an almost unrecognisable Evan Dando with cropped, spiky hair.

Its release was greeted with almost universal acclaim from The Lemonheads' hipster Boston friends.

Listening to the record now, it's clear that even at that early stage, Evan's songwriting contained many of the subtle twists and nagging hooks that were later to become his trademark on 'It's A Shame About Ray' and 'Come On Feel The Lemonheads'. Both the title track itself and the bitter 'Don't Tell Yourself It's OK' resonate with a raw charm, a naive simplicity which only comes about when a band are playing music for the sheer love of it.

Ben Deily's tracks, meanwhile – like the superlative punk love song 'Uhhh' (which is sung very much in the style of late-Seventies Irish punk-popsters, Stiff Little Fingers) and the early Lemonheads classic 'Fucked Up' – are equally as memorable. Even the handful of average hardcore tracks ('Rat Velvet', a lame cover of 'Amazing Grace') sound fine, recorded with such youthful enthusiasm.

Strangely, two of Ben's poppiest songs which were recorded at that time – the okay-ish 'Sad Girl' and far superior 'Ever' – didn't surface until 1989's 'Lick' album. Perhaps it was because they were *too* melodic for Jesse and Evan's hardcore sensibilities back then. That's certainly what Ben believes.

'I don't know why they weren't used,' Deily mused aloud to *Record Collector*.

Left: John Strohm; Above: Husker Du

'They were poppy and zappy, but at the time Evan and Jesse didn't like poppy and zappy.'

Although the record was high on the energy and punk quotient, early Lemonheads sounded far closer to the thrashy melodiousness of The Ramones rather than the all-out noise attack of their DC 'straight edge' contemporaries such as Rites Of Spring. Evan's songs – even at their most rudimentary and angriest – have always contained melodies.

'We were super naive back then,' Jesse recalls. 'But we were in a band for totally the right reasons [the music] – there was no conception we could make money off it. When we recorded "Hate Your Friends", we knew that it was exactly the kind of record we wanted to make.'

And it was a fine way to start their career.

The Replacements, a major early influence

★★★★★★ ★★★★★★★

Creator

The Blake Babe

iven a helping hand by MTV, who showed the video for the track 'Second Chance', 'Hate Your Friends' continued to sell steadily during the rest of 1987. And, although Jesse and Ben were attending Harvard, the band found time to play the odd couple of dates along the East Coast.

'It was very disorganised,' the bassist recalls. 'I'd call up a place, borrow my mom's station wagon with the U-Haul trailer and off we'd go for the day. We were very reliant on friends' floors back then.

'The Lemonheads were definitely much more democratic when they started,' he continues. 'Ben and Evan might have been singing and writing the songs, but I was the person who was booking the shows and organising the recording sessions. In fact, up until Atlantic started showing an interest in us, I pretty much managed The Lemonheads. There was a real balance in the band.'

An old friend of the band confirms this: 'Jesse was the one who held things together, who did most of the organising,' he told me. 'Evan was much more quiet and withdrawn. He was genial, but aloof – Jesse was the practical one. He'd be the one out buying toilet paper and food for the apartment while Evan was lying out on the sidewalk on Newbury St [Jesse and Evan shared a pad there during 1989/90].'

'Everyone had very distinct personalities,' Jesse says. 'All I remember about Ben was that he really annoyed me. He was just this really irritating preppy punk guy who would get on everyone's nerves. Evan was more of an unstable freak, so you had to make him think he was deciding everything.'

In the summer of 1988, the band started recording 'Creator', with John Strohm (Blake Babies) on drums and Tom Hamilton at the controls. This time, however, they didn't find it such plain sailing.

'All our hipster friends who had been so supportive over the previous 18 months joined the Lemonheads backlash around then,' recalls Jesse. 'It was the first local one we ever suffered, although people like New York's Gerard Cosloy [then editor of punk fanzine *Conflict*, now boss of the Atlantic-funded Matador label] had always hated us. In his review of the single "Hate Your Friends" he called us an A-Ha [mid-Eighties teen-pop trio] lookalike band. People have always felt threatened by Evan's good looks or hated us for that reason.'

Jesse and Evan out on the highway, Illinois, 1988

Evan with the Blake Babies in the late Eighties

The backlash occurred despite the fact the album contained what Jesse calls 'three of the finest songs Evan has ever written': the abrasive, sprawling 'Die Right Now', the turbulent 'Clang Bang Clang' (later re-recorded on 'Lovey' as 'Left For Dead'), and 'Out'. They were the only Dando compositions on what is undoubtedly the weakest album The Lemonheads ever released.

There were the ubiquitous, fairly pointless cover versions: Evan's cool reworking of the Charles Manson song 'Your Home Is Where You're Happy', and a faithful cover of Kiss's tribute to Chicago's Cynthia Plastercaster, who attained a certain amount of infamy by preserving rock stars' private members for posterity in plaster. (Kiss, incidentally, were never asked if they wanted to have their cocks preserved. The Lemonheads were – and did!)

The remainder of the songs on 'Creator' were written by Ben Deily and are unremarkable pop-punk fare – it didn't help matters that Mr Deily was, at that point, going through an infatuation with American poet Emily Dickinson.

Already, it appeared that The Lemonheads were being led in two different directions. On the one hand, Ben was writing poppy, reasonably straightforward, romantic numbers. On the other, Evan was definitely becoming fascinated by the darker side of the Sixties culture he grew up with – and his songs, often tortuously noisy affairs, reflected this.

(It wasn't until 1991, when Evan had finally lost all hope of The Lemonheads ever succeeding and went to Australia, that he rediscovered how to mellow out and finally began to write the uptempo, light pop songs The Lemonheads are famous for.)

'"Creator" is definitely the most embarrassing Lemonheads record,' Jesse groans. 'It totally sucks. That album was what started the backlash which has continued to the present day.

'You could see the split forming even while we were recording the album. Evan would be quoting from Charles Manson ["Clang Bang Clang" was named after the

Jesse Peretz and Evan Dando at Cape Cod, 1988

first three lines from the Manson song "Big Iron Door"] and, meanwhile, Ben's name-dropping Emily Dickinson on the sleeve credits. Although, to be fair, I think Ben's infatuation with romantic poetry came about because at the time he had a girlfriend who looked as if she'd stepped straight out of a Walt Disney musical.'

'Ben got a little bit weird,' Evan laughs. 'He started liking Keats, Yeats, whoever. Yeah, Ben had a really early Yeats infection.'

To support 'Creator' The Lemonheads did a small tour across America, but already Evan was becoming increasingly fed up with the band's lack of focus.

'After "Creator" came out,' Ben told *Record Collector*, 'Evan started quitting the band on a regular basis. Throughout The Lemonheads' history, he was never satisfied with some-one and would always be complaining about them. I may be wrong, but I flatter myself for being the only member Evan didn't want to get out.' (Evan and Ben roomed together during this period – phone number 876-PUNK.)

'He was always coming up to me and saying, "We gotta get rid of that drummer, he sucks,"' Ben added, 'or "Jesse's a shitty musician, we gotta get rid of him."'

'I didn't like our early records,' Evan told *MM*'s Carol Clerk in 1993. 'I wasn't satisfied. All the other kids were going to Harvard and I just wanted to be a proper drop-out musician.'

'It was fun,' Jesse says now, 'but it was also really pretty miserable. Things really started getting to be a bummer. Evan's always been prone to bad moods, to being a little manic depressive – and he would always get frustrated at me and Ben not being better musicians and having other things going on in our lives.'

Evan was by then a far more accomplished musician than the other Lemonheads. And, despite the fact he would often be working in a restaurant or somewhere similar, there would be plenty of moments when he wasn't doing anything at all. And thus frustrated that the band weren't going anywhere.

This inequality between the band's respective positions in life would continue right throughout their Taang! years – right up to 'Lovey', in fact, which was recorded during Jesse's final few months in college.

Matters came to a head onstage at a club in Cambridge when a stroppier-than-usual Evan Dando decided to play the riff from Guns N' Roses' 'Sweet Child O' Mine' instead of all his usual guitar solos.

No one said anything on the night, but as far as everyone there was concerned, The Lemonheads were finished. Evan wouldn't play with the band for another eight months.

Jesse and Ben sloped off back to Harvard to continue with their college degrees, and Evan went across to join John Strohm in Juliana Hatfield's Blake Babies.

EVAN AND JULIANA

Evan Dando and Juliana Hatfield first met in a pizza shop when they were both about 19, the day after Juliana first saw The Lemonheads supporting then local hardcore heroes, Volcano Suns. That would've been around the latter part of 1986.

'I liked them,' Juliana told *MM*'s Carol Clerk in a joint interview the pair did with the paper, November 1993.

'I thought they were really earnest and cute, and the songwriting was really outstanding. We met Ben that night, but not Evan. I remember thinking Ben was . . . wow! It took me a while to realise Evan's brilliance.

'The next day, I went into this pizza shop in Boston with a friend,' she continued. 'It was a Saturday, so it was very crowded. Evan was in front of me in the line with his girlfriend. I introduced myself. I said, "I liked your show last night." Then I told him the name of my band, and he said his mom

had come to see us. He came to see us after that.'

'I thought they were something special and wanted to be friends with them,' Evan recalled. 'They obviously liked The Velvet Underground like I did.'

They met again the next time The Lemonheads played, supporting a local satanic heavy metal band. Juliana brought along flowers which ended up being strewn around the club – in sharp contrast to the headlining band who were singing about death, gore and the devil onstage.

'That night, they gave us a lift home in a van that said "The Lemonheads" on the side,' Juliana remembered. 'Then Evan came

Evan Dando and Juliana Hatfield: two of the new generation of guitar hero pin-ups for the 'alternative' kids

'Just good friends' – Evan Dando and Juliana Hatfield, November '93

over to where the Blake Babies were living and hung out. Evan lived in that place, The Condo Pad, for a while. My mom owned it and we paid rent to her.'

'I lived in people's living rooms all throughout my early twenties,' Evan explained, 'and that was one of them.'

By the winter of 1987, the friendship between Evan and Juliana – helped by the connections between their respective bands – had blossomed into an all-out romance, according to Jesse. He told me that, during this whole period, Evan was

going out with a girl called Emily, but everyone knew that he was going and spending the night and fooling around with the virginal Juliana Hatfield.

'Evan, at times, has admitted having sex with her,' Jesse reveals, 'but other times he'd come back and tell me what a freak virgin she was. She was obviously really infatuated with him from the beginning, tied up with her admiration for him musically. Somehow, their friendship became very intense very quickly. As did Evan's relationship with the Blake Babies.'

Evan and Juliana, in all fairness, tell the story very differently:

'I had a crush on him,' she admitted, 'but I was cool about it. I didn't make a big deal about it, and that's good cos it's meant we've been able to be friends for a very long time. Sometimes people are too intense, and then things blow a fuse.'

'I have this theory that because we knew we had to pursue our own things and we'd be apart so much, I knew we should never start going out,' Evan explained. 'I never asked her to go out with me. I never knew if she would. But it wouldn't have been good to be attached.'

It was during this period that Evan took over bass-playing duties with Blake Babies full-time, helping them record the poppy and charming 'Slow Learner' album (then available in the UK on Billy Bragg's Utility label and well worth tracking down).

However, it quickly became apparent that playing second fiddle, even to one of his closest friends, wasn't going to satisfy the restless Dando.

'Evan kept having problems with the Blake Babies,' explains Jesse. 'He was continually frustrated because he wasn't playing his own songs. Maybe at one point he and Juliana were flirting with the idea of working together as a creative unit instead of her with John Strohm, but presumably Juliana didn't like that. She's always been a real workhorse at getting things done and Evan isn't at all. He was a real fuck-up.'

Evan eventually left Blake Babies in January 1989. Out of the blue, The Lemonheads had been offered a free trip to Europe the following summer, courtesy of tour promoters, Paperclip. It was too good an opportunity to pass up.

Evan reformed the band, with himself as drummer. It might have seemed a weird move at the time, but he was fed up with not having control of the band and wanted to prove that he could do anything within the band he chose.

'I had to take the opportunity,' explained the singer, 'but, from that moment on, I thought, "Fuck it, this'll be my band." I felt bad when I left the Blake Babies cos I missed hanging around with them so much, and I loved playing bass.'

The end of the original Lemonheads was very near.

Juliana flashes her cash with the Blake Babies

★★★★★★★★★★★★★★★

Lick

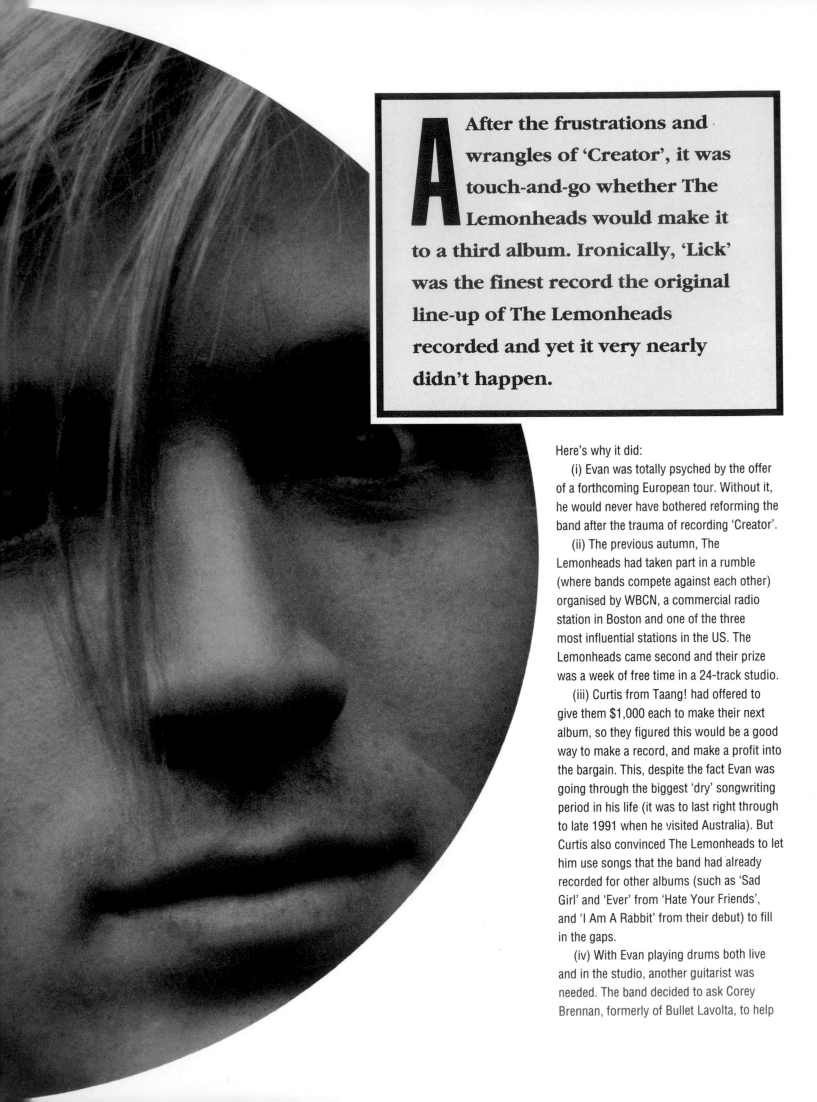

After the frustrations and wrangles of 'Creator', it was touch-and-go whether The Lemonheads would make it to a third album. Ironically, 'Lick' was the finest record the original line-up of The Lemonheads recorded and yet it very nearly didn't happen.

Here's why it did:

(i) Evan was totally psyched by the offer of a forthcoming European tour. Without it, he would never have bothered reforming the band after the trauma of recording 'Creator'.

(ii) The previous autumn, The Lemonheads had taken part in a rumble (where bands compete against each other) organised by WBCN, a commercial radio station in Boston and one of the three most influential stations in the US. The Lemonheads came second and their prize was a week of free time in a 24-track studio.

(iii) Curtis from Taang! had offered to give them $1,000 each to make their next album, so they figured this would be a good way to make a record, and make a profit into the bargain. This, despite the fact Evan was going through the biggest 'dry' songwriting period in his life (it was to last right through to late 1991 when he visited Australia). But Curtis also convinced The Lemonheads to let him use songs that the band had already recorded for other albums (such as 'Sad Girl' and 'Ever' from 'Hate Your Friends', and 'I Am A Rabbit' from their debut) to fill in the gaps.

(iv) With Evan playing drums both live and in the studio, another guitarist was needed. The band decided to ask Corey Brennan, formerly of Bullet Lavolta, to help out. He'd left his previous band to go to Rome for a year to study classics. Insiders agree that Corey, more than anyone, helped get The Lemonheads back on their feet again – simply because being around him was so much fun.

'We all totally loved him,' Jesse says fondly. 'He was one of the funnest guys, a total geek with a high-pitched voice and an awesome heavy metal guy who played totally fast guitar.'

A WHRB DJ with big thick glasses and a great sense of the ludicrous, Corey was into punk rock with the precision of a PhD history student. He knew everything – the more obscure a band was, the more into them he'd be. Corey was the ultimate rock geek/trainspotter who, in the most rock of rock situations, would start drawing classical analogies and using his heavy vocabulary to put his point across. And his vocabulary included seven languages!

'The Lemonheads formula is to be as rivative as possible,' he told one rviewer, straight-faced. 'When we're ng songs, we take a Stiff Little Fingers, acements and an early Husker Du re and play them simultaneously on dif ont stereos. We turn the volume up real loud, and we all take notes. That resulting jumble is called The Lemonheads. That song "Mallo Cup" [from "Lick"] is "Suspect Device" [Stiff Little Fingers] mixed in with an unholy dose of The Replacements' "Don't Ask Me Why". And no, don't ask me why.'

'The whole Italian song ["Cazzo di Ferro"] on "Lick" was just whipped out by him and Evan so quickly,' a still awestruck Jesse recounts. 'They borrowed the chord progression of another band he was in, wrote the lyrics about this show *Ironside* [a TV programme featuring a cop in a wheel-chair that the band were obsessed about at the time] and set it in hip Roman slang.'

FIASCO

Recording 'Lick', however, was a fiasco from beginning to end.

The band were originally meant to be in the studio for a week, but the time stretched to two months as Evan's songwriting block became worse and worse.

'We were so casual about it,' recalls Jesse. 'We were only really doing it for Curtis and so that we could each make a thousand dollars. We promised we'd play a couple of shows to help promote it, but we hadn't actually reformed.

'At that point it was fun, but I could take it or leave it. I wanted to do films. I wasn't looking for a rock project at all. I didn't know what Evan and Ben were going to do and I didn't really care.'

There was a problem on the production front, too – all the previous Lemonheads records had been recorded with Tom Hamilton, a real sweet, up-and-coming record producer from Boston. But the band had decided they wanted something different so they flew over Terry Kapzman – who had supposedly recorded with The Replacements in the past – to Boston. Later they had to get Tom back in to remix some of the songs.

Work on 'Lick' started in February 1989. It soon became apparent that there were problems. While recording his vocals for '7 Powers', Ben refused to let Evan and Jesse in the studio and made them stand out in the corridor. Jesse and Ben got into a big fight halfway through the sessions and Ben quit.

It was the first time Ben had quit the band. Things were eventually patched over, but everyone present knew it wouldn't last.

Evan Dando, blessed with the looks of a bleached surfer god, Cape Cod, '88

Ben wasn't too interested in going along with what anyone else was doing, and Evan and Jesse were becoming increasingly embarrassed by what they viewed as Ben's corny songwriting techniques.

'Ben, Evan and myself were arguing all the time,' Jesse told *MM*'s Push in the paper's first-ever interview. 'We tried to keep the whole thing pretty casual, but even so, every day, the rows went on and on and on. I'm really surprised that we managed to get the fucking album finished.'

It was all the more remarkable then, that this 'mishmash of different demo tapes and weird shit' (plus a couple of new, bonafide pop songs) made for such a great album.

'The bumpy nature of "Lick" is not only a further testament to the seditious spirit of Boston's Lemonheads,' Push wrote at the time, 'it also marks a burgeoning maturity. A work of brittle caresses and fractured carousels.'

Perhaps the band's very casual approach to their work stood in their favour, giving the album a lightness of touch which it wouldn't have had otherwise. Certainly it's always held true that with Evan's songs the more effortless they seem, the better they sound.

The two songs which really made the album work as far as their fans were concerned were two Dando compositions – the velveteen, morose 'A Circle Of One' and the plaintive 'Mallo Cup', both of which stand up against anything he's ever written. Ben's sizzling 'Anyway' is pretty damn good too.

Those poppier songs sat in pleasant contrast to the tumultuous guitar pyrotechnics of 'Cazzo di Ferro' and the more straightforward 'Sad Girl'.

The song which was to make the biggest impact, however, was the band's electrifying version of Suzanne Vega's 'Luka'. Originally recorded for 'Creator' as a joke, the band hadn't bothered releasing it before because they were so embarrassed by it. Thrown onto 'Lick' at the last moment, it ironically became The Lemonheads' first chart hit when it was released as a single in the summer of '89.

Melody Maker made it a Single Of The Week, writing '"Luka" is straightforward, old-

Corey Brennan (right) joins the band, 1989

fashioned awesome', going on to compare it to similarly essential cover versions by US hardcore bands, such as Husker Du's 'Eight Miles High' and Dinosaur Jr's 'Just Like Heaven'. (The sleeve features a photo of Jesse's sister, incidentally.)

'Luka' was the record which made the majors, specifically Atlantic, finally sit up and take notice. The band were indifferent to its success, partly cos they were on tour – and thus unaware of it – and partly cos they were embarrassed by the fact it had taken a cover version to finally gain them the attention they felt they deserved.

(Oddly enough, it took another cover – The Lemonheads' piss-poor, lacklustre, jangly take on Simon & Garfunkel's 'Mrs Robinson' – to be the record which finally broke The Lemonheads as major artists, both home and abroad. And, like 'Luka', the song got added to American copies of The Lemonheads' then-current album after the album had already been released.)

BEN QUITS

'Lick' was to be both the last album the band recorded for Taang! and the last featuring all three original members.

According to Jesse, Ben had become very attached to his girlfriend and kept wavering between whether he was going to tour Europe with the band or not. When he did eventually quit the band, after a string of disastrous hometown shows during which Evan sang his parts from behind the drumkit, it was through a combination of the band pushing him out and him wanting to leave.

'Ben was being such a weird loser at the time,' Jesse recounts. 'He decided he couldn't go away for too long, so we said we were going to go without him. And that's where he stepped off for what turned out to be the final time.'

'During "Lick", the band went through a real tumultuous period,' David Ryan, their current drummer, explains. 'They weren't talking much. The tension between Evan and Ben had just got too competitive. Both of them have always had that strain in them – perhaps it comes from prep school. Ben said, "As of now, I think this band is creatively bankrupt." So they kicked him out, and he kind of quit as well.

'By the time I joined the band,' continues David, 'Jesse and Evan weren't even talking to Ben. He was suing them to not play any of his songs from thereon.'

(Ben told *Record Collector* that he had originally hired a lawyer to get his share of the royalties.)

'It shocked all of us that he'd do something that belligerent and baby-like,' the drummer adds. 'He spent a lot of money on a lawyer just to ensure this one point, when all he really needed to do was just ask us. So, to this day, we don't play any of his stuff.'

Ben's departure marked both the end of the first phase of The Lemonheads and also the start of Evan's growing status as a songwriter. Until Ben left, the band were continually being pulled in two directions – a state of affairs that sometimes worked, but more often didn't.

With him gone, Evan was given space to develop, to follow his own muse – through his infatuations with Manson and Gram Parsons, old-fashioned uncomplicated pop music and recreational drug use – to lead The Lemonheads where he saw fit.

Which was eventually to be Australia in early 1991, and the recording of the masterly 'It's A Shame About Ray'.

On Tour

When it became clear that Ben had gone for good, Evan decided once and for all that he wanted to play guitar – much to Jesse's relief, despite the fact that they would have to find a replacement drummer for the impending tour.

'Evan's always been passive/aggressive,' Jesse says. 'Saying, as he did at the time, that he just joined The Lemonheads to play drums was part of that. He was being totally retarded, because he's always been able to play guitar better than Ben or Corey or myself. So anyway. There we were needing a new drummer, with this all-important European tour due to start in two weeks!'

Beggars can't be choosers though – as the band were shortly to find out, much to their chagrin.

The drummer they eventually ended up with was a chap called Mark – a very dour character, by all accounts, with long black dyed hair. None of the band can actually remember Mark's surname, but they soon nicknamed him Budola.

There was something very disturbing and scary about him, but it wasn't until the actual day the band left to go on tour, late in May 1989, that Jesse got his first 'taste' of what the new drummer was really like.

The night before they left, Jesse's 'awesomely cool mother' threw a barbecue for all the party (including Bullet Lavolta who would be supporting The Lemonheads on tour), and Budola ended up going home with Jesse's friend Jill.

Jesse takes up the story:

'The next day we were on this totally packed plane to Amsterdam,' Jesse tells me. 'I had Evan crammed in to the left of me, Budola on the right. The plane's taking off, I'm dozing off to sleep, when suddenly Budola nudges me. He sticks two fingers under my nose and says, "Do you want to smell your friend Jill?" That was the first insight wc had into his character.'

Later on during the tour, The Lemonheads were offered a show opening for Living Colour in Brussels, in front of what would have been their largest audience to date. Unfortunately, the night before in Germany, Budola had left with some girl after the concert (as was his wont) and had forgotten to inform anyone where he was headed.

The band spent four precious hours the next morning driving through the streets yelling his name. By the time they arrived in Belgium, Living Colour were already playing. So the wiles of Budola's willy meant that The Lemonheads had missed thcir first chance to play in front of 3,000 people.

To make matters worse, all through the journey their tour manager had been telling them about one particular hotel in Brussels she'd stayed at previously which was infested with crabs. Having blown out the concert, the band were left with no choice. Corey ended up sleeping with all his clothes on and his jacket buttoned up tight, while Jesse and Evan went downstairs and slept on the pool table.

Despite these trials, Jesse remembers the tour as 'the funnest time we ever had, second to when we went to Australia for the first time. It totally revitalised the band.'

It was during this tour that the band first became aware of one of Evan's more peculiar habits: sleepwalking. The singer had been prone to somnambulism during his adolescent years, but it wasn't until they toured Europe that the other members of The Lemonheads really became aware to what extent.

One particular incident occurred in Nijmegen (near Amsterdam in Holland), where the band were staying at a hippy commune situated in an old abandoned monastery. Everyone was asleep in their bunk beds, with Evan at the top, when the singer started thrashing about, leaping from bunk to bunk.

Just another day on the touring treadmill

Fulham Greyhound, London, 30 June '89

STRANDED ON TOUR

Back home, The Lemonheads began their first comprehensive tour of the US in July 1989 (without Corey, however, who'd gone back to concentrate on his PhD and marriage). It was to be both their last for Taang! and the end of Budola's short sojourn with the band.

He quit right in the middle of the tour, causing the band to spend a huge amount of money on flying a replacement from Boston to California.

'After playing Seattle, we drove to Portland, Oregon,' Jesse told me. 'Everyone except for me and Dan [Estabrook, long-term Lemonheads roadie] had been snorting speed all night, so when we got into town they crashed all day. When Budola woke up he was so weird, telling us all to fuck off. Anyway, we got to the club, and the bar next door looked like a warzone. It had been bombed the previous night. To compound matters, the sign over the club read "Welcome To Downtown Beirut".

Eventually, the band's manager at that time (who, strangely enough, also happened to suffer from the same affliction as Evan) managed to restrain him and get him safely back in his bunk.

'I have these night terrors, whatever, demons,' the singer explained to *Melody Maker*'s Caren Myers the following year. 'And I get up and run into a wall. The night before we came on our tour, I ran down the hall and knocked a painting off the wall and broke this huge mirror. Then I grabbed this candelabra and ran into the living room and stood there waiting for someone to come out.

'It gets to be very exhausting sometimes,' he continued. 'You don't get very great sleep like that.'

The same year, while staying at a strange little hotel in Basel, Switzerland, his manager woke in the middle of the night to find that the singer had gone from his bed. Realising he must be out sleepwalking, she went to look for him.

Eventually, after a long search, she found him at a pet zoo near the hotel, sitting in the middle of a rabbit pen, with a bunch of bunnies around him. He was petting them and talking to them.

'It was *so* cute!' she crooned to me.

The Fulham Greyhound represented a genuine English 'pub gig' for The Lemonheads

Recalling the 'garage band' tradition of Sixties American rock, rehearsals were as vital as gigs in the band's development . . .

'Budola turned around and said, "You guys all fucking hate me, I hate all of you and this is the last fucking show I'm going to play with you." So that night he took a plane back to Boston. We never figured out what the problem was – even if we did make fun of him constantly, because he was such a buffoon. Like he'd do things like buy soap in New York instead of crack.

'So that stranded us, right in the middle of the tour. We blew out two shows, drove to San Francisco where we had some time off,

and tried to find a drummer to finish the tour with. Our manager flew out some guy from Boston, who was terrible, and we tried out a bunch of people. Then, after three days, Budola came down from the speed, flew back out and we finished the tour.

'That was it, as far as us and Budola were concerned. Except that the following spring, when we were trying to finalise our deal with Atlantic, we placed an anonymous advertisement in the local paper for a new drummer. And Budola was one of the people

who applied! Our manager spoke to him on the phone for about five minutes before she realised.'

It was the same advert that was to bring current-day drummer David Ryan to The Lemonheads' attention.

DAVE DONUTS

David Ryan had actually met Evan a couple of years before he joined The Lemonheads, while he was working as a pastry baker in a donut shop.

. . . the danger was, things could get so laid back it was clearly time to go home

Fulham Greyhound, London, 30 June '89

Playing clubs like the Greyhound marked a return to the punk ethos of small venues . . .

. . . a long way from the stadium rock that had dominated the established scene

Evan was playing bass for Blake Babies at the time. After late night rehearsals, the band would drop by for donuts and coffee from the guy they knew then only as 'Dave Donuts'.

'Evan seemed a nice guy,' David says of their first meetings. 'I don't know whether he tipped well or not – cos I used to give them the stuff free; they'd sneak in after the place was closed – but I imagine he would've done. I didn't even know his name then. I'd seen The Lemonheads play pretty often round Boston, but never connected the face.

'I knew John and Freda [Blake Babies] a little better,' he continues. 'They were all regular guys, normal nice white kids. Then again, the guy out back was dealing drugs and there would be tons of pimps and prostitutes around. People would be getting into knife fights while I was trying to bake donuts. The Blake Babies were milksops in comparison.'

Born 20/10/64 in Fort Wayne, Indiana, David Ryan spent his first 18 years growing up in a conservative midwestern (Illinois) family. His parents were very supportive of his musical aspirations when young – they didn't even bat an eyelid when he used to regularly practise eight hours a day. Maybe it helped that they were both involved in musical careers themselves – his dad worked for a local radio station and played bass, while his mother used to sing jingles for local businesses.

David was given his first snare drum at 10. It was a choice between that and playing clarinet in the school band. He chose the snare, cos it sounded cooler and louder. But he didn't start getting totally serious about drumming until he discovered jazz when he was 16 years old.

He moved away from home just after his parents split to travel round America for a couple of years, forming his first band in New York City. At the age of 20, he started studying English at the University of Massachusetts in Boston, supporting himself by bar-tending and making donuts.

'I learnt my craft from this ex-con called Mario,' he told *MM*'s Caren Myers in June

Evan Dando in Europe, 1990

1990, during The Lemonheads' mini-tour of the UK to help promote the 'Favourite Spanish Dishes' EP.

'He was wanted in 12 different states for armed robbery and some kind of horrible assault. He had a tattoo on his penis that said "Kiss me", or so I hear! This guy was one of the best bakers in the world; he was unbelievably fast. He was really intelligent, but also incredibly dangerous. I had a knife pulled on my throat one night at the bakery and he saved my life. Anyway, he taught me and I actually started to surpass him towards the end, which caused a lot of bitterness. Then, one day, the cops figured out who he was and he disappeared.'

LIFE WAS GOOD
When David first got asked by The Lemonheads' manager in the spring of 1990 if he wanted to try out as the band's new drummer, he'd been trying to quit playing drums for a while. He needed to concentrate on his studies.

But, he figured, if Jesse still had a couple of terms left to run at Harvard University, maybe their schedules might coincide. The Lemonheads didn't seem too serious a concern back then.

One day, a roommate came home and told David he'd seen Evan at a club and had mentioned his name to the singer as a prospective Lemonhead. The very next day, someone came along and gave the drummer a lift to what was, in David's words, 'a dumpy house in the lame, college part of town', where Jesse and Evan lived.

Of the two, David remembers Jesse being the friendlier. Evan was altogether more distant. Maybe he was just tired – by this point, the pair had auditioned more than 40 drummers. David started playing and, after a while, noticed that both Jesse and Evan had big grins on their faces.

'Which was kind of nice,' David recalls.

Seven days passed before Jesse called with the good news: David was now officially a Lemonhead. Two weeks later the band departed for a mini-tour of Europe (during which they would cover Madonna's 'Borderline'!)

A record company insider who met them on that tour remembers the band as friendly, charming, sophisticated East Coast kids.

'Jesse and David hung out together all the time. They shared common interests – books, art, poetry,' the source revealed. 'Evan was scattier, more rock 'n' roll. Even then he had his "big hunk o' love" thing down [his Boston friends nowadays fondly refer to Evan as "His Blond Loveliness"].

'It was a fun time. They played a show at the Zap in Brighton in late May and afterwards we all got drunk and started singing Gram Parsons and old punk songs.

'Life was good.'

FAVOURITE SPANISH DISHES

Allegedly, the day that Jesse called David to tell him he'd passed the audition was the very same day that The Lemonheads' contract with Atlantic was signed.

According to David, this put a strain on everything: 'Evan was going through a lean patch as a songwriter. He's never been very prolific, but maybe he felt pressured all of a sudden. This was when indie bands were being snapped up by majors. But instead of trying to sign one band and stick with them, they'd sign 12 and split the money 12 ways. The Lemonheads were just another piece of line in the net to the record company.'

In the UK, a cover version of Mike (The Monkees) Nesmith's 'Different Drum' was due to appear on Roughneck. As soon as the band signed to Atlantic, the company rush-released the track in the US as part of the EP, 'Favourite Spanish Dishes'.

Yet another *MM* Single Of The Week, it incorporated the country-eqsue, unrequited feel of the Linda Rondstadt version with a healthy dose of screaming feedback.

'As fearlessly wonderful as I could ever dream for,' I wrote then. 'It starts in a similar, melancholic vein to the original but, by about the second chorus, something has gone seriously awry with the guitars, screeching and scorching and tumbling through speakers in the background.'

The plaintive 'Paint' on the B-side was about 'yearning and longing', according to Evan. 'It's a metaphor for a person,' he told Caren Myers. 'I read this book when I was a child that affected me greatly about this nice happy industrious crane that worked and then got put down into this pit and left all alone. So I remember just being sad about the crane. Inanimate objects induce sadness in me like nothing else.'

Snapped on the road

The other song was 'Ride With Me' (later to be appear on 'Lovey'), one of the most beautiful, most aching songs Evan has ever recorded. Ironically, it incorporated both images of Jesus and various phrases the Manson family used.

Evan explained to *Zip Code* in November that year that it wasn't the Manson murders he was into, more that he empathised with how the killer felt.

'He's just fascinating,' the singer stated. 'He's an inexhaustible source of curiosity to me. Although his ideas are deliberately idiotic and simplistic, there is something in them. Forgive me for saying so, but he had so much pain inflicted on him by society. His mother was a whore and his dad left before he was born . . . One of his first acts of aggression was at a birthday party and suddenly when nobody was looking, he grabbed all the presents and brought them back to the house and burned them all in the backyard. He'd been left out of everything, and was trying to get his revenge.'

'He has an interesting view on the world cos he was always the outcast,' he told Caren Myers. 'I don't like the way he tried to get people to do things, though. I'd much rather stay uninvolved with anybody . . . empathy is definitely the right word.'

The Lemonheads in Stuttgart, Germany, 1991

Lovey

In April 1990, the new line up of Evan, Jesse and David began work on The Lemonheads' fourth album, 'Lovey', at Fort Apache, Cambridge, this time with Paul Q Kolderie at the controls.

Despite rave reviews from the British press at the time (*MM* called it 'The Lemonheads at their most murderously charming'), it was a patchy affair. Somewhere along the line, The Lemonheads seemed to have lost their reasons for being in a band.

Songs like the aforementioned heart-tugging 'Ride With Me' were unnecessarily beefed-up, while the opener 'Ballarat' was a horrendous mêlée of wailing guitars and the terrified screams of children. (Its title was taken from *The Family*, the story of the Manson family. Ballarat was the final place the Mansons went to when things were closing in on them after the killings.)

'(The) Door', meanwhile, sounded like *The Scorpions* for Chrissakes!

And what the hell was that wacky answer-phone message (recorded by actress friend Polly Noonan) doing placed at the end of that track. You don't buy a Lemonheads album for the comedy content, do you?

There were highlights too, however – the bitter, almost spoken word 'L'il Seed', the classic Dando jangle of 'Half The Time' and the faithfully mournful cover of Gram Parsons' 'Brass Buttons' among them.

'My admiration for Gram Parsons goes back a long way,' Evan told *Sounds* in 1990. 'I love all his work, from The Byrds through the Burritos [Flying Burrito Brothers] and his solo stuff. But that song is the one I've been itching to do.'

Mostly, however, such moments were swamped by a production that made The Lemonheads sound as if they were trying to aim for the *Keranggg!* market. This was before grunge hit the big time, remember.

And then there was 'Stove', a sweet, odd-ball little love song written for a . . . stove! Inanimate objects DO induce sadness in Evan, it seems.

'That song's just the diary of a day,' Evan told *MM*'s Dave Simpson. 'You get so used to something, some object in your house and then, when it's gone, you don't really notice it unless it's sitting outside on the sidewalk for the garbage-men to take away – a real sad image. I told a friend of mine about it, and he encouraged me to write the song.'

All in all, though, 'Lovey' didn't sound as if it was a particularly happy record to make.

'It was not a good time,' Jesse confirms. 'That whole period was definitely when Evan began realising how much control he had over the band. When we were in the studio recording "Lovey", he'd wait till we'd gone home and go over our parts. That was the beginning of the downward

shift as far as I was concerned, when I really started to shake out of the whole thing emotionally.'

'"Lovey" was the album that nearly got Lemonheads dropped from label,' says David. 'The A&R people who signed us had quit and we were stuck with people who didn't give a shit about us. That's when it really started falling apart, when the pressure really hit, cos that's when Evan started realising it was a choice between either playing music or pumping gas for a living.

'Recording it was a nightmare,' he continues. 'Jesse and I were trying to finish up school. I had my finals right in the middle of recording. So I went in, did my drum parts, then two weeks later the producer called me and told me to come in urgently.

'Apparently, Evan had decided he was a superior musician to both of us, and had decided to start from the bottom up and play all the tracks again. Jesse had it worse than me. Evan wanted to re-record all his tracks. It bust out in fisticuffs at one point – Jesse threw a chair at him. That was the beginning of the end for us.'

Performing live in Stuttgart, Germany, March '91

THINGS JUST FELL APART

Things started going from bad to worse in The Lemonheads camp. At the end of an arduous European tour timed to precede the album's release, during which Evan split up with his longterm girlfriend Hannah (who was selling T-shirts for the band at the time), The Lemonheads disbanded.

Jesse had walked out of the band in Leeds, right in the middle of the UK leg. Although he returned, that was it as far as he and David were concerned.

'It was mainly due to the tour, I guess,' Evan explained to *Melody Maker* at the time of the split. 'That tour must have been the most gruelling we've ever done . . . you know how a tour can get. I dunno, things just . . . fell apart.

'It started off with the recording of the album,' he continued. 'The two guys were in school at the time, finishing off their university studies, and so I played the bass and drums on some songs and so . . . I think that basically made them upset.

'I can understand why, but I wanted to get it right, y'know? They didn't really have the time to do it and maybe I was too lazy to teach them exactly what I wanted, so I just went ahead and did it! I guess I was sowing the seeds of discontent.'

'There's no figuring Evan out sometimes,' says David now. 'I could say a lot of ugly things about what made him do what he did – like he's an egomaniac or psychopath or something – but that's not the whole story. He was going out with a girl at the time who was telling him he was a god and I think that got to him. He does have a tendency to take flattery to the extreme. That, combined with pressure and nerves, compounded the whole situation.'

When I met up with the band in April '91, Evan informed me that he'd been falling head-over-heels in love with his girlfriend and that had created even more friction.

'At one point,' he claimed, 'Tina [the tour manager] called my girlfriend a "fucking cunt of a whore" and she punched her!'

Evan was later to write the song 'Hannah And Gabi' (from 'It's A Shame About Ray') about the split.

'Gabi, this Australian model, allowed me to get away from Hannah and I felt disappointed with myself,' he told *Vox* magazine in March 1993. 'But I didn't really want Gabi, either – she was a symbol of what I was missing. And before that there was this girl, Louisa, who I got away from. I want to stop getting away from everybody. I want to find the right girl.'

Hannah was, in fact, the last girl that Evan seriously went out with. Part of the reason for this is clearly down to the restrictions of being a pop star, while part is down to fall-out from his parents' divorce. As Evan told *Melody Maker*'s Sally Margaret Joy at the end of 1992.

'It's been a year-and-a-half since I've had a girlfriend,' he informed her, 'because I gotta get myself together. It's hard. I'm not gaining any ground. I always had girlfriends, right from second grade. But I was always excited about meeting new, exciting, differ-ent people all the time. And girlfriends would

Posing for the cameras . . .

hard to really ask someone you don't know that well what it's like to sleep with you. I don't want to get too analytical about it.'

Is that because you're scared they might be wanting something different out of it?

'Well,' he paused. 'They can't find me, anyway.'

TRAPPED ON TOUR

It wasn't only girl trouble which caused the split, however. Evan was getting far too possessive about his own songs for David and Jesse's liking.

'When you write a song, you have the whole song in your head,' explains the drummer, 'and when the band don't play it exactly like that, you flip out. That's what Evan was like then. He forgot that after a couple of weeks of playing the song as a band that your vision changes. You can hear the drums Evan plays on "Lovey" ["Ride With Me", "Half The Time" and "Stove"]. They're definitely a little bit sloppy.

. . . in Stuttgart, March '91

be getting way too wrapped up, and they'd get all bitter and sour and pissed off, and that made me so angry. I'd be, like, "How can you deprive me of this thing where I wanna meet new people?" and, of course, I was a terrible flirt. I like to think love can be spread around, and is totally infinite.'

Evan has since contradicted himself on this point.

He informed *Just 17* in February '93 that he wasn't into one-night stands. 'It's no fun,' he said. 'I need affection, and there's no affection in one-night stands.'

But in the very same month he told me he thought, 'People need to have sex at least twice a month. You wear a condom and stuff, and you're careful. But it's more like a need, a thing you have to do. It's more of a chemical than emotional thing.'

I asked him whether that would be the same for the girls he'd slept with.

'I don't know,' he hedged, momentarily surprised. 'That's a good question. I'd love to imagine what it's like for them, but it's

Hannah, Evan's last 'serious' girlfriend

'But shit, it was his prerogative. He always came back down to earth after a while. Sometimes he needed a kick in the jaw, but then he'd be okay.'

It always seemed that, around then, The Lemonheads could have turned into a solo project at any moment, that Evan may even have wanted it that way and was forcing a situation where a decision to stay together or split up would become inevitable.

'That was something that was going through his mind a lot, I think,' David says. 'Some of it was because he admired J Mascis [Dinosaur Jr] and J could play drums. At the time J was turning to Lou [Barlow, old Dinosaur bassist, now frontman with Sebadoh] and whoever played the drums and yelling at them that they sucked in front of 2,000 people. And that's precisely what Evan did to us on that UK tour which we quit halfway through.

'Finishing that tour was a nightmare, the worst time of my life,' he continues. 'There we were, trapped in a van and hotel room

together, no one talking to anyone else, for over two-and-a-half months. That girlfriend didn't help matters, either.'

Although the three band members did manage to pull together and complete the tour, the respite was only temporary. The problems had never really been resolved and as soon as the tour was over the three went their separate ways, leaving 'Lovey' to succeed or fail without them.

Evan Dando, the man with the voice AND the looks

TRUCE

Perhaps inevitably, with no band to promote the album, 'Lovey' flopped. It sold around 11,000 copies, compared to 30,000 for 'Lick', their last album for Taang!

Although some UK industry insiders loyally insist that if Atlantic had bothered releasing 'Half The Time' as a single The Lemonheads would have hit the UK charts a couple of years before they did, it seemed that The Lemonheads couldn't get much lower.

Sell-out dates headlining at the Town & Country Club in London with support from fellow Bostonians Buffalo Tom (The Lemonheads sold T-shirts from their van outside) didn't seem to count for much either.

After Jesse and David quit the band in mid-1990, Evan hired a couple of musicians from Kentucky (Ben Daughtry from Squirrelbait on drums, and Byron Hoagland on bass) to fill the gap.

It wasn't a success.

Everyone liked the new members, but they simply weren't suited to The Lemonheads – either musically or temperamentally. The autumn US tour to promote 'Lovey' was a nightmare. Both musicians would frequently get plastered after the shows – on one occasion, Byron turned up in Washington State with the shit kicked out of him. It was the first taste Evan had of how irresponsible musicians can be while touring.

'They were way too weird,' the singer told me in April 1991 during the band's short European tour to promote 'Patience And Prudence', an ill-conceived four-track EP which included jaunty cover versions of New Kids On The Block's 'Step By Step' (!) and the schlocky Fifties song 'Gonna Get Along Without Ya Now', plus an acoustic 'Stove'.

Ill-conceived, because it was The Lemonheads' third cover version-for-single in a row, making it seem like they were merely covers band (one music paper termed them 'a Barron Knights for a barren generation'). Ill-conceived, because it sounded as if it'd been knocked together one rainy afternoon when the band had nothing better to do.

'They didn't take it seriously,' Evan continued, 'which wasn't the main thing as I didn't take it too seriously either, but they made an outrageous play of the whole thing and made goofy faces the whole time. Plus, the bass player had a beard, which was unacceptable.'

For once, Evan was the one who had to keep his shit together and that freaked him out. He soon realised he'd made a mistake in letting Jesse and David go.

Drummer David Ryan, working up a sweat and dressing for the occasion

Most observers agree that The Lemonheads' tour of Australia in the summer of 1991 proved to be the most significant event in Evan's musical career, leading to the band's breakthrough album 'It's A Shame About Ray'.

A cheesecake Evan Dando looks cool for the cameras in a hotel bedroom

Although The Lemonheads were only touring in Australia for a few weeks, it was during this period that Evan met most of the people who were to provide both the antidote for his songwriting block and the inspiration for 'It's A Shame About Ray', including both future songwriting partner Tom Morgan and future Lemonheads bassist Nic Dalton.

'Nic was playing with this band from Sydney called The Hummingbirds, who were supporting us on tour,' recalls David Ryan. 'He was filling in for his ex-girlfriend Robyn who was pregnant with the singer of The Hummingbirds' baby. So he was actually touring with the father of his ex-girlfriend's baby! I remember being totally shocked – it seemed like the most fucked-up situation I'd ever heard of. But once you know him better you realise it's not like that.

'He's just one of the funniest guys I've ever met,' the drummer continues. 'He makes me laugh continually, but he's totally natural. He never makes jokes. It's his peculiar behaviour that does it. He's got this perplexing mixture of boyish innocence and amazingly cynical adult to his character.'

Evan Dando, possessor of a voice that can sound huggable and wistful all at once

HALF A COW

Nic Dalton, the only boy among a family of six, grew up in the mundane surroundings of Australia's capital, Canberra. Born on 6/6/66 (or so he claims), Nic was a hyperactive kid who veered towards outright naughtiness. He got expelled from the school where he studied English and art for throwing a milk bottle through a window and smoking pot. He'd always been loud, the class clown, the boy who'd get on better with girls than his own sex.

A big Beatles and Velvet Underground fan, Nic's one of life's natural record collectors. He got into punk at the age of 12.

'Every time we go on tour, he seems to buy 100 new singles,' David recounts in awe. 'He's always shipping stuff home.'

Nic was 14 when he first picked up a guitar, but it wasn't until 1990 he began to take playing music seriously. It was then he moved to Sydney to start his own label – and, subsequently, record store – in Glebe, a suburb of Sydney. He named them both Half A Cow, after a picture he'd had in his possession since school.

Half A Cow's debut release was an album of charming lo-fi pop from his then-girlfriend Robyn St Clair's The Love Positions. Since then, it has released records by Sneeze

(Nic and Tom: brief, haphazard pop), Smudge (Nic, Tom and Nic's current girlfriend Alison Galloway: US-style frenetic punk-pop) and Godstar (Nic, Alison and sometimes Evan: thrashy summertime beach pop). Among others.

Nic's never sent records out to magazines or record labels, however. He's never been too interested in fame, as he told *Sky* magazine, December 1993.

'I didn't do this thinking we would all become stars,' he explained. 'I did it because I love music and I love putting out records. But it's definitely been a trial and error process – even now we're still learning.'

Ironically enough, for a label which hardly bothers promoting itself and would never press up more than 500 copies of a record, ever since The Lemonheads came into Nic's life, various Half A Cow acts have found distribution deals right across the world.

The shop, which sprang out of a cool Sixties Canberra bookstore run by his parents, sold all manner of hip items – from records by the UK's My Bloody Valentine to books by William S Burroughs to the indigenous comic book, Fox Comics.

Its exterior – a dull, scruffy brown, enlivened by a yellow picture of half a cow which looked as if it was painted by someone high on good drugs – was covered with peeling posters for underground Australian bands. The shop itself was up a flight of battered stairs.

Tom Hamilton with Evan Dando, Europe, '90

MIRACULOUS RESURRECTION

The Lemonheads soon found themselves gravitating towards the portals of Half A Cow, attracted by its good-time slacker vibes.

Nic recalls his first impressions of Evan.

'I met him backstage at a concert we played together,' he says. 'I remember he was wearing khaki baggy trousers, leather shoes and a T-shirt. He seemed a funny, friendly guy – certainly not strange or crazy or any of those things he's meant to be now.

'I didn't know what to expect of them live, as I'd only heard "Different Drum" and "Luka",' he continues. 'But I thought they were really good. They reminded me of a

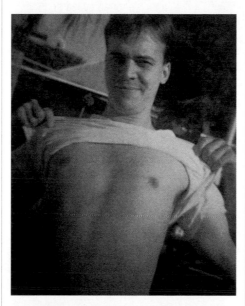

David Ryan, 'sunbathing' in Australia, '91

band I was in at the time called The Plunderers who would mix up punk rock and country songs. The Lemonheads were the first band I'd seen who were attempting something similar.'

At this point, The Lemonheads were well on the road to becoming a mournful country band, reflected in the songs they chose to cover ('Night Time' by Alex Chilton, any number of Gram Parsons tracks). Evan's ongoing depression meant that he preferred to sing melancholy, sad numbers – numbers that suited the solo treatment. It seemed like The Lemonheads wouldn't last much longer.

'When we first met, Evan had told me he was going to do a solo country record,' Nic reveals. 'No one knew what was happening with The Lemonheads, beyond the fact they were probably going to split up.'

After meeting up with Tom and Nic, however, The Lemonheads went through a near-miraculous resurrection. Evan, in particular, found his enthusiasm for creating music totally rekindled by meeting up with the people around Half A Cow. As an insider so buoyantly explained, life soon became 'fun fun fun all the way'.

'Half A Cow just inspired me more than anything that's come along in a long time,' was how Evan simply put it.

Tom Morgan and Alison Galloway, Australia, '93

SURFING PARADISE

Who were these people who were to play such a big part in Evan Dando's life, right up to the present day?

First up there was Tom Morgan, the 'big and lazy' songwriter from local Sydney band Smudge, who was later to co-write most of 'Come On Feel The Lemonheads'. Smudge were then best known for their tongue-in-cheek tribute to recalcitrant Go-Betweens' singer Grant McLennan,

called (amazingly enough) 'Don't Wanna Be Grant McLennan'. He and Nic also played together in a band called Sneeze. The pair sheepishly asked Evan if he'd mind contributing to their debut 40 the sofa.

Then there was Alison Galloway, the drummer with Smudge, Nic's current girlfriend, later to form the inspiration for 'Alison's Starting To Happen' (from 'Ray'). As the song goes, 'You're the puzzle piece behind the couch that makes the sky complete.' It was initially written about one time she was on ecstasy, but Evan turned the song round so it became 'more of a love thing'.

There was Tom's roommate Nicole, the girl who stars in 'My Drug Buddy', a song written about 'scoring speed on King Street in Newtown', according to Nic. ('Ceiling Fan In My Spoon', meanwhile, was written about precisely that, inspired by an incident in a cafe round the corner in Emmerdale.)

There was Robyn St Clare, the then-pregnant bassist for

Left: Nic Dalton, NYC, '92; Above: Dando

The Hummingbirds who Nic was standing in for. She'd written 'Into Your Arms' (later to appear as the first single off 'Come On') about Nic for her band The Love Positions' debut album. Her baby Milo, meanwhile, was the subject of 'Rockin' Stroll', and featured heavily in its video.

'If I write songs about people it's because people leave their imprint on me and I'm just trying to describe that imprint,' Evan explained in a video interview. 'It's like I'm dusting a fingerprint that's on me, and by writing a song about it, it becomes clear to me what it is. It's me trying to give back something to someone who's given so much to me. And that's so fun to do.'

'That tour definitely mellowed Evan out,' says David. 'He found people who lacked pretensions there and that helped to reaffirm his belief in music. All that crowd were

Mellowing out with friends in Australia

creative, even if it was in a strange way. There was hardly anyone out there who couldn't be creative off the top of their heads. Like, someone would pick up a crayon by chance and then spend the whole day drawing with the crayon onto walls.

'The creativity seemed inbuilt into their culture. Also, for the first time in a long while,

Sydney-based band Smudge

Evan was being showered with praise from a bunch of cool people. That sealed it – that and the weather. He loved the weather!'

'We went disco-dancing, took a lot of ecstasy and generally had a good time,' laughs Nic. 'I remember one day when we were catching a bus to go and record the Sneeze record, Rob Young of Radio Birdman [local old-time punk heroes] was on board. Evan was so excited! He went through the park yelling, "I met Rob Young, I met Rob Young!" The Lemonheads were the first people from overseas I ever swapped addresses with.'

'We hung out on the beach,' remembers David fondly. 'It was a surfing paradise. Everyone just sat around and did this whole hippy love-fest thing.

'I remember one day Nic carved a big X into his chest,' he recalled. 'He walked around with a towel wrapped round his head, waving what he called his "Ooga-Booga Stick" from on top of this big pile of rocks. Life was good.'

A likeness of the Ooga-Booga Stick can be seen etched into the CD of the six-track 'Chemicraze' EP by Godstar.

JESSE QUITS

In August 1991, Evan, Jesse and David headed out to the UK for what turned out to be Jesse's last tour with the band. For their final British date at the Mean Fiddler, Corey Loog Brennan joined them onstage.

'The Lemonheads are so mighty because they understand rock 'n' roll is here to be treated with all due irreverence and disrespect,' I wrote in a review of the show. 'This is rock as rock should be played: with humour, with vivacity, with spunk, with LIFE!'

(Diehard Lemonheads fans might recognise the latter part of the above quote from a sticker used to advertise copies of 'Ray' when it finally appeared.)

The reasons for Jesse's departure were three-fold. One, he was starting film school that autumn. Two, the band appeared to be going nowhere. And three, there had always been some weird competitive streak between him and Evan, dating right back to childhood, a love/hate relationship.

'It's ironic,' says David now. 'When we first headed out to Australia, it seemed like the band didn't have any chance of survival.'

It was only after Jesse had gone and we started to record "Ray" that Atlantic seemed to suddenly start caring about us.

'Then again,' he continues, 'it was just when "Nevermind" was starting to break big and all the major companies were scrambling to find their own pseudo-alternative band. Obviously, Atlantic woke up one morning to realise they had one on their own doorstep.'

Two months later Evan decided to return to Australia, this time by himself, where he stayed with Nic and Alison for a couple of months.

'It's a good jarring thing, to be so far away,' he told me in 1992. 'I like being under pressure, otherwise I find it hard to motivate myself. I wish I could build things, or cook, or sculpt, or something, but I can't. The only thing I can do is write songs, but that's pretty satisfying too.'

It was then he asked Nic to join The Lemonheads (the bassist eventually joined on July 1st 1992) and to help him write songs for a new album. Nic was busy, so he told Evan he should hook up with Tom Morgan.

Two days before Evan left, Tom wrote half of the track 'It's A Shame About Ray'. Evan's songwriting block was about to be cured, once and for all.

CRAZY

Back home, however, shorn of all his new-found friends and musical allies, Evan quickly found himself as depressed as at any time in his life. Or maybe it was just all the E wearing off. Whatever the reason, he decided to check himself in with a psychologist sharpish.

'It really helped me get out of depression for a while, and to realise I wasn't as crazy as I thought,' he told *MM*'s Carol Clerk in his joint interview with Juliana, two years later. 'It was nice to be able to talk about how desperate I felt. I was just immobilised. It was a chemical thing. I think it might have had a lot to do with drug abuse making me depressed. All the doctor did was say, "You might want to take a break from all the drugs

Could this be a trend? Nic poses in party frock . . .

for a while and you might feel better," and I did. And that was a long time ago.

'I went to Australia in October 1991 to write songs for "It's A Shame About Ray",' he continued. 'When I got back, I'd finished it. It was all about the things I'd done down there, and I was still there, even though I was back home in Boston. I couldn't make head or tails of it. That's when I went to this shrink.

'I loved it down there in Australia. I hated being home. I was depressed. It was

freezing. Nash Kato from Urge Overkill came to our house, and there was this little black-and-white TV in the corner with a Walkman on top of it. He said, "It's a home entertainment centre."'

'He bought a bottle of Beaujolais over, and there was no corkscrew,' added Juliana. 'So he had to push the cork down, and there were no glasses. We had to drink it out of the bottle.'

'He cheered us both up a lot,' finished Evan, smiling.

Shame About Ray

Recording on 'It's A Shame About Ray', The Lemonheads' fifth album and the record which was to finally catapult them into the big-time, began in the first few months of 1992.

Evan with brat-pack buddy Johnny Depp, Los Angeles, 1992

Finding himself without a bassist, Evan asked old friend and then-roommate (address: Brainerd Road, Boston) Juliana Hatfield to step in. Blake Babies were just about splitting up by that point, anyway. The band spent a month in Boston rehearsing, then flew out to LA in March to start recording with renowned producers, the Robb Brothers (previously responsible for Rod Stewart and David Bowie, among others).

David remembers the time vividly.

'The day we arrived,' he says, 'was the first time LA had had any floods for a long time. All the streets were pouring with water. It looked like Armageddon had hit early. It was the most gorgeous day of my life. All I remember are the palm trees, and how everything seemed to be really tropical.

'We got a totally deluded introduction to LA, much like experiencing Hollywood in the Twenties must have been. The studios we

recorded the album in were the same place as where Ray Charles and Sammy Davis Jr recorded "Candyman" at, just in the conference room where we used to have meetings round the big glass table.

'We hung out with all these famous filmstars, including Johnny Depp. At the time I didn't know much about him except his on-off relationship with Winona [Ryder], but even that blew me away. I remember us all going up to his house somewhere near Magic Mountain. It overlooked Julian Lennon's pad, the roof of which still had "Piss Off" written on it for all the helicopters. It was a whole different world. Every day was like a mad party.

'I just remember hanging out at the apartment we were given, feeling blown away, phoning home to friends and playing rough mixes, nearly crying with all the excitement. Unfortunately, that world

Relaxing at Evan's old school, June '92

sound a lot like pukey old skinny tie power pop to some of you, and as new and thrilling as Pavement to others . . . I suggest you purchase this album and get cured quick. Try not to resist.'

The whole record had a warm, clearly ecstasy-influenced feel to it, which reflected Evan's description of Australia as 'one big Valium'. The Robb Brothers tried toning down The Lemonheads' grungier extremes by incorporating acoustic guitars, and the gambit paid off in trumps.

There was so much to explore, from the big hug-in sound of 'Rockin' Stroll' to the upbeat insurgency of the gorgeously truncated 'Bit Part', which featured Juliana screaming the intro. From the frantic rush of 'Kitchen' (Nic's one songwriting contribution) to the breezy, perfect pop of the Dando/Morgan-composed title track.

'The title comes from this guy in Melbourne, Australia, who everyone calls Ray,' Evan explained to me in July '92. 'He made me start to think Ray could be a name for everybody, so "It's A Shame About Ray" could be about anybody. It's a pretty grey, indefinite kinda thing, but it's also very specific. I'm not sure if the person singing the song is Ray himself, or someone who knew him.'

Also featured were the drop-dead beautiful, narcotic 'My Drug Buddy', the topsy-turvy 'Ceiling Fan In My Spoon' and the misleadingly breezy 'Confetti', the song Evan had written about his parents' divorce.

'A lot of my songs are about comforting myself,' Evan revealingly told Sally Margaret Joy later on that year.

And let's not forget the magical cover of 'Frank Mills', which tied in with the ancient Lemonheads tradition of only covering songs which had originally been sung by women.

'To hear Evan Dando sing lines like, "I love him/But it embarrasses me/To walk down the street with him/He lives in Brooklyn somewhere/And he wears his white crash helmet",' I wrote in a review, 'is to truly appreciate how wonderful and tantalising pop music can be.'

doesn't actually exist, as we found out to our cost the next time we came out.'

TRY NOT TO RESIST
Between Evan meeting Tom Morgan in Australia, the band's experiences in LA and the Robb Brothers' production, the unique sound of 'It's A Shame About Ray' came about.

Melody Maker's Sally Margaret Joy described it at the time as 'fantastically immediate'.

'"Rudderless",' she went on to write, 'swallows your heart whole into its warm mouth. It aches with the inexpressible. The melancholy, loneliness and languor of adolescence seem to resonate in the thrum of acoustic guitar. Evan Dando has perfected the sound of teenage longing . . . "My Drug Buddy" trails a rapturous surge of love on a stroll from the candy store to the phone booth. You're there. You can feel the warmth of the pavement coming up through your shoes . . . "Alison's Starting To Happen" will

It was an unashamedly magnificent album. And just 29 minutes long! What more could a lover of pop music ask for?!

JUST A COVER VERSION AWAY

Nic joined The Lemonheads just in time to help them tour the US in July 1992 in support of their just-released record, supported by a recently gone-solo Juliana Hatfield.

A live *MM* report of the show from Toronto stated that 'Evan Dando is so beautiful he makes your teeth ache; a total dude and he knows it . . . he's gonna be a lot more of a star real soon. Tonight, Evan Dando and the other two guys play for two hours; they play bass and drums, and he plays with us like plasticine.'

Evan and David, Europe, fall '91

Amsterdam, '93

soundtrack written by Simon & Garfunkel) on video that the album finally started to sell. A band was needed to help sell the film to a younger audience, and so The Lemonheads were asked to re-record 'Mrs Robinson' from the soundtrack.

They recorded the song in a couple of hours in Germany and hurried through a video to help support it. The worst Lemonheads single ever (and Nic's debut vinyl appearance for the band, incidentally), it was also notable for having possibly the strongest B-sides Evan has ever recorded – 'a small constellation of acoustic sighs,' as the *Melody Maker* so

He was 'an Elvis Costello with cheekbones', as another critic put it.

For The Lemonheads, genuine star status was but a cover version away.

The first single to be issued from the album, its title track, despite being issued with exclusive live and acoustic and outtake tracks, flopped. (It's well worth picking up, however, to hear Evan's acoustic cover of Sneeze's brilliantly mournful 'Shakey Ground' and the decidedly dodgy original of 'Dawn Can't Decide'.)

It wasn't until someone gained the rights to re-release *The Graduate* (the Sixties film starring Dustin Hoffman, and featuring a

Evan on the band bus, Europe, '91

poetically put it. Three songs, all coming in at under two minutes, including far superior, gentler versions of two songs from 'Come On' – the winsome 'Being Around' and the yearning 'Into Your Arms'.

It was November 1992 and, all of a sudden, The Lemonheads had a (minor) worldwide hit on their hands.

The song later got added to the soundtrack of *Wayne's World 2*. As with 'Luka' a couple of years before, however, the band had mixed feelings about attaining success with a cover version.

'I remember being a little bit saddened that a song which had already been digested for years, spoon-fed to the public, had made people finally buy our album, which has got some really good songs on it,' David laments. 'It's a shame this lame-ass song had to be the one for America. Also, it was kind of bad because it got added to "Ray" and that made 13 songs on the album, and instead of touring for five months, we ended up on the road for over a year. We hear Paul Simon hates it though; that's pretty cool.'

To celebrate his belated success, Evan Dando performed a solo acoustic show at London's Ronnie

Wearing Johnny Depp's finger watch, '93

Scott's in the final month of 1992. (Thus prompting further speculation that The Lemonheads were about to split once more!)

It was an astonishing performance, as Evan held a crowd of industry cynics spellbound for over two hours. (There was an equally large crowd of fans kept waiting patiently outside for the duration in a rainstorm, who left infuriated when the singer finally departed the club, hopping straight into a limousine.)

'Live, alone, strumming big clumsy chords on a guitar that spends the set trying to break free of its strap,' the *Maker*'s Andrew Mueller wrote, 'Dando makes the truths sound pretty eternal. He cradles his delicate, precious songs like an ape cradling a kitten . . . A wonderful afternoon. If only more could have seen it.'

RELAXED AND JOVIAL

'Mrs Robinson' was followed in January 1993 by 'My Drug Buddy' (one of Evan's all-time favourite Lemonheads songs, along with 'Big Gay Heart' from 'Come On'). The

New York City, 1992

label quickly flipped the single to make 'Confetti' the A-side when it became apparent that no radio station was going to play even the poppiest of songs with 'Drug' in the title.

It was during this period that Jesse shot the 45-minute-long 'Two Weeks In Australia' video, which featured all the band's new friends. There's even a cameo appearance from Johnny Depp in a video for the single 'It's A Shame About Ray' that the actor directed himself. 'Mrs Robinson', mean-while, was filmed along a canal with Evan wearing the Gram Parsons T-shirt he'd been given on one his earlier visits to Australia.

There's a segment dedicated to Nic's guitar, with the story of The Lemonheads etched onto its reverse, including scenes where Juliana Hatfield is kicking a ball into Crater Lake and Nic is waving the Ooga-Booga Stick around.

Other videos featured include the one for 'Half The Time', featuring the post-'Lovey' Lemonheads line-up of Evan, Byron and Ben brandishing pumpkins and chainsaws, and a great acoustic preview of 'It's About Time' from their future album.

'Back when I was very unreasonable,' Evan explained on tape, 'I met this girl called Juliana . . . and this is me and Tom's attempt at writing her autobiography. This song is done in the style of Juliana Hatfield.'

The song has since been interpreted as an open invitation from Evan for Juliana to lose her (much-touted) virginity with him. Like, 'It's about *time* . . . '

Evan later coyly dismissed this suggestion by pointing out that the 'song veers off at the last minute. It's just celebrating Juliana, that's all.'

With various other videos recorded at in-store acoustic sessions and live shows, the video documentary is a great chance to see the band in a relaxed and jovial mood, with some candid commentary from all involved.

GLAM-GRUNGE

By this time, the critics were becoming split right down the middle about the worth of The Lemonheads, perhaps misled by what was then already becoming popularly accepted as Evan's persona: the slacker, the airhead, the drug-addled loser.

Some preferred his earlier forays into college rock: 'The sound of any talented artist in a dilemma is just more arresting than that of someone who's got the self-confidence thing sussed,' wrote *MM*'s Sharon O'Connell about the reissue of 'Lovey', comparing it favourably to 'Ray'.

Some were starting to be won over by his pop sensibilities: 'I'm growing to love Evan's featherweight pop grunge, despite or very possibly because it sounds so un-late 20th century,' a critic wrote about 'Confetti'.

And some simply couldn't fucking stand the sight of him: 'Mediocre, middling, air-head rock . . . spectacularly non-fascinating reflections from an extraordinarily uninteresting psyche.'

One wonders quite how much of all this was deliberately brought about by the singer himself, however.

'The *Daily Star* ran a story saying: "Pop idol Evan Dando has turned his back on the rock star lifestyle and is sleeping rough in the back of a Mustang",' Evan told me during our interview in February '93. 'They painted this strange bohemian fantasy of my life.

'I'm starting to believe it,' he half-joked. 'I think I might take it on as my persona, my "Dippy Dando" persona. I'm just going to roll with it. Apparently, I don't like hotel suites, I just like to take a bus and pitch a tent in a friend's garden and eat at cafes. And it says I'm planning to emigrate to Australia, because America is no longer a safe place to hitch around.'

I asked him what he thought it was his record company saw in him.

'We're their glam-grunge band,' he laughed. 'No, I don't know what they see in us. All I know is they want me to smile into the camera . . . Oh yeah, man, I'm happy to do it.'

Whatever the critics thought, though, it seemed as if nothing could stop The Lemonheads now.

A reissue of the 'It's A Shame About Ray' single followed, and became the next hit – mostly due to some shameless packaging from the record company (great acoustic and live versions of various songs from the album on the flipside), it has to be said. 'Shouldn't this be Album Of The Week?' the *MM* cattily asked.

'Ray' (the album) went on to sell in excess of 500,000 copies. It was time to record the follow-up.

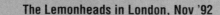

The Lemonheads in London, Nov '92

Feel The Lemonheads

In July 1993, The Lemonheads headed out to LA to begin recording their sixth album, 'Come On Feel The Lemonheads', with the Robb Brothers at the controls once more.

Whereas 'It's A Shame About Ray' had seemed to be almost a solo Dando record in places, this new album promised to be more of a band outing and thus easier to record. After all, the line-up of Dando, Dalton and Ryan had been on the road for almost a whole year by now. It quickly became clear that things wouldn't be so simple, however – even with Tom Morgan co-writing eight of the songs on the album.

Even with the promise of guest appearances from such star names as king-pin funkateer Rick James, ex Go-Go's chanteuse Belinda Carlisle, Gram Parsons' side-man Sneaky Pete, and old-time collaborator Juliana Hatfield.

Even with a few hits under the band's collective belt.

The band were under substantial pressure from the record company to capitalise on the partial success of 'Ray'. Evan was increasingly coming under intense media scrutiny. And, last but not least, it soon became apparent that LA was not the same city as when The Lemonheads had last visited it.

It had changed. And not for the better.

'It was like the city was the polar opposite of what it had been,' David told me. 'There was something about LA that was really bad this time out, that wasn't happening before. When people used to tell us we were good during "Ray", we believed them. This time, their plaudits were starting to ring a bit hollow, a little insincere. We realised they were only telling us that so we'd make a good record.

'The city had turned bad on us. Instead of floods, fires were happening this time. All of the friends we had made out there, or had been around, while we were recording "Ray", had disappeared. And we were under even more pressure this time. We knew that people were having these meetings, saying that we'd better not fuck this one up.

'When we got out there, I hadn't even heard half the songs. Any time we'd been given off, Evan would be out doing press somewhere. We were being pressurised to make a better record than "Ray", which should have been easy because we'd been touring for so long, but was hard because Nic and I didn't know the songs.

'All the external pressure came out in our behaviour. After being in the studio, I'd go back to my room and then just sit and stare. I remember spending whole days just staring at my wall. I don't know why I did that. The pressure made us all flip out a little. Evan was depressed a lot of the time, not that he ever showed it in public.

'You can only hear people telling you how great you are so many times a day before you want to punch someone in the mouth.'

HOLLYWOOD

Nic Dalton remembers it slightly differently. There again, it was Nic's first time in Hollywood.

'Harry Nilsson came in, smoked some pot and played us some new demos he'd just done,' he enthuses, thrilled at the memory of meeting one of his childhood heroes. 'Mostly, they were songs looking back on his Seventies days, kind of like The Beatles meet Ween. They sounded lo-fi and cool, especially coming from this middle-aged guy with a paunch.

'Me and David were there for five weeks, laying down the basic tracks. It was fine. We did about all of the 14 songs really fast, then we'd just sit around the rest of the day talking. Did we hang out with any celebrities? When you're in LA, it's bound to happen.

'We met Lita Ford [ex-Runaways]; that was cool. She's a good LA person to meet. The Robb Brothers would tell us funny

stories from the Sixties, and made sure we didn't use anything digital or false, just cool instruments.

'It was fun recording the album, but the rest of it wasn't so great – like having to stay in LA. It's a horrible place, really.'

PURE BONAFIDE POP

All the more remarkable then that the album which finally appeared in October 1993 turned out to be so beautifully, and not fatally, flawed.

An uncertain Jim Arundel, reviewing it in the *Maker*, called it 'all over the place'.

'For a record that's undoubtedly expected to be their zillion-shifting consolidator, it's

Rejected cover for 'Come On' album

oddly disjointed,' he wrote. 'It opens with the obvious stuff, the singles, the songs featuring Juliana Hatfield high in the mix . . . but then "Come On" starts to become sloppier, rowdier and noticeably more bizarre than its predecessor.'

Frankly, he didn't know what to make of it – and no wonder. For 'Come On Feel The Lemonheads' is an incredibly schizophrenic album.

The first side almost sounds like it was intended to be 'Ray II', with its near-constant stream of pure, bonafide, rush-of-blood-to-the-head pop – the nonchalantly resigned 'The Great Big No', the innocent romance of 'Into Your Arms', for example. Side two, meanwhile, is increasingly punctuated by long silences, studio chat

and extraneous noise, finishing with a free-form piano track ('The Jello Fund'). As a reflection of Evan's troubled state of mind at the time, it couldn't be more apposite.

There are even two versions of one song: the brilliantly fucked-up 'Style'. The first is all upbeat and self-assured, the other all drowsy and resigned, with Rick James singing soulful LA falsetto in the background. 'Don't wanna get stoned/Don't wanna get stoned/But I don't wanna not get stoned,' a weary Evan laments, in a painfully aware appreciation of how all-pervading his chosen lifestyle had become.

According to David, however, the song's subject matter isn't as clear-cut as it might first seem.

'Evan changes his story about the meaning of "Style",' the drummer tells me, 'but frankly that song is less about drugs than it appears to be. It's written about those moments when you're feeling indecisive, but you don't want to do anything else. It's also about people coming in and telling you you're great – hence the LA hook-word at the end of each chorus, "Style!" It's definitely a passive/aggressive thing. The content also stems from "My Drug Buddy", cos Evan always wanted that to be a single, but the radio stations wouldn't accept it because of its title.

'That's another song which isn't really about drugs. "My Drug Buddy" is more about friendship, and lonely friends. The drug motif is the shotgun on the wall, it's the prop for the song.'

Then there was old favourite 'Being Around', which some people felt Evan had deliberately thrown away by making it so bouncy and jaunty, and the devil-may-care Belinda Carlisle duet, 'I'll Do It Anyway', which had the same accusation thrown at it.

As far as the latter song goes, David agrees with the critics.

'It's one of the most annoying songs I've ever heard,' he says. 'Evan originally wrote it for Belinda to record for her album, but it arrived too late for that. We didn't have enough songs for "Come On", so it ended up on the album. We don't play it live.

'We initially did it like a Rolling Stones/Replacements-type tune, which helped it a little. Then, when Nic and I left, Evan did all those overdubs, got Belinda in and ended up with the album version. It doesn't sound like much of a Lemonheads song to me. I'd much rather have heard Keith Richards play on it.'

David also disagrees with me that the whole song is one big drug reference ('I'm still a girl/It's just a horse/And I've got the reins': horse = heroin). In fact, he claims the thought never even crossed his mind until I suggested it.

'I never thought about the heroin reference,' he states. 'I thought that line was really funny, actually – Evan singing this neo-feminist thing as a guy. But that's Evan all over. He's always covered songs which were written from a female perspective – like "Luka" or "Different Drum", or even "Into Your Arms" from the new album.

'That's why "Mrs Robinson" is so bad, cos it doesn't fit in. It was like an in-joke with us to cover songs by female artists, and once you take away the joke, you're just left with a bad punchline.'

In other places on the album, there's genuine heartbreak and tears: Evan and Tom Morgan's tribute to Juliana Hatfield, 'It's About Time'; the by-now almost obligatory paean to an inanimate object, the moving 'Favourite T'; the self-doubt of 'Down About It'.

Then there was the awesome, dewy-eyed 'Big Gay Heart': either a moving bid for the pink vote with its country-esque, Gram Parsons mannerisms, or a patronising, cynical cash-in – depending which side you're on.

'Evan called me when I was down in Boston,' recalls David. 'He was hanging out in a house which was being rented out by a friend at the time. It was a very tasteful mansion, but with a lot of homoerotic paraphernalia around. He called me at 9am, not having slept, to say he loved me or something – he does that quite a lot – and I remember him ranting about this big gay house he was in, saying, "Hey, have a big

gay day." It was around this time that he started injecting the word "gay" into everything, for its happy connotations.

'There was a certain amount of irony behind writing the song in a country fashion, because that's the music which is most often associated with rednecks and hence gay-bashing.'

Then there was the straightforward adrenaline rush of the loopy 'Dawn Can't Decide' and unashamedly hedonistic 'You Can Take It With You'.

They were both songs which reflected Evan's increasing unhappiness with the media glare which surrounded him, and the 'Grip And Grin' world he found himself trapped within – as was the more overtly cynical, yet strangely compassionate 'Paid To Smile'.

'That song is right up our bum,' David explains. 'It's the LA thing, and it's also kind of everyone's problem. If you're in showbusiness or any similar job, and you don't like the people around you, you feed into that. Basically, what Evan is saying in that song is that we are all cigarette girls when it comes down to it.'

Ultimately, 'Come On Feel The Lemonheads' has an effortless pop sensibility to it, helped greatly by Juliana's frequently spine-chilling back-up vocals and Evan's refusal to ever treat even the harshest of subjects less than humanely.

All the disparate threads come together to give the album a power and passion far beyond its simple bubblegum comparison points (David Cassidy? *Please*) or even more critically-acclaimed artists such as . . . well, fill in your own grunge rocker.

A truly, truly classic album.

SOME THINGS NEVER CHANGE

The album was preceded by the Robyn St Clare-composed single, the outrageously soppy 'Into Your Arms'.

The critics, by now, were out in force.

'I'm sorry, but The Lemonheads are just the most overrated bunch of lukewarm strummers to drift out of the States and into our line of vision in many a long

moon,' wrote the *Maker*'s man. 'I mean, aren't they?'

Clearly, their fans didn't agree.

Backed by a truly inspirational cover of Cole Porter's 'Miss Otis Regrets' (which infuriated as many people as it made swoon), 'Into Your Arms' made a sizeable impact on the charts.

It was quickly followed by the Juliana tribute, 'It's About Time' – 'spindly tripe,' as one critic called it.

On the contrary, I think it's quite, quite charming.

The B-side to that single is almost as odd as the album itself: incredible acoustic takes of 'Big Gay Heart' and 'Down About It', plus a third version of 'Style'. This one showcased Rick James warming up for the song in rehearsal (Rick was jailed soon afterwards for his part in some sex scandal).

Evan had style, and he knew it.

For the picture on the flipside, the record company simply used an old defaced press shot of the band, with horns coming out of each member's head.

It seemed like releasing a single – even in late 1993 – was as effortless, as un-time consuming as that for The Lemonheads.

Some things never change.

Evan in Australia, spring '93

My Drug Buddy

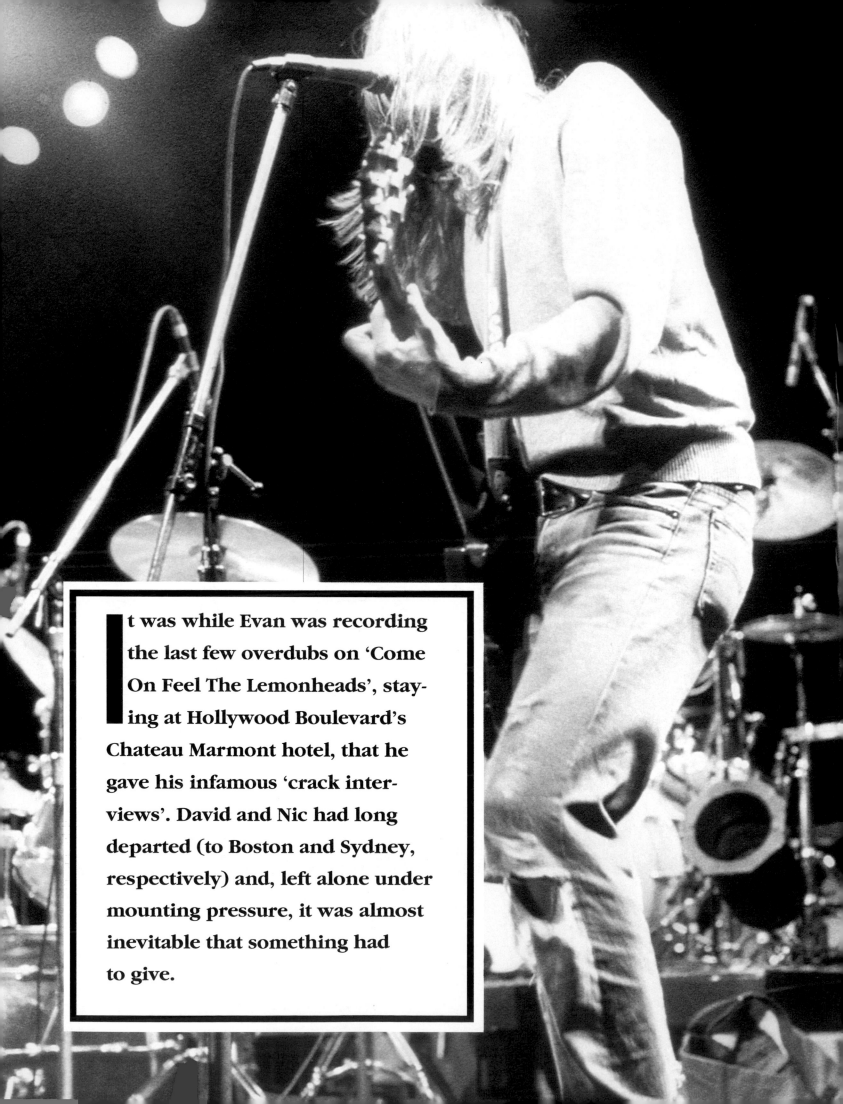

It was while Evan was recording the last few overdubs on 'Come On Feel The Lemonheads', staying at Hollywood Boulevard's Chateau Marmont hotel, that he gave his infamous 'crack interviews'. David and Nic had long departed (to Boston and Sydney, respectively) and, left alone under mounting pressure, it was almost inevitable that something had to give.

Evan gives impromtu free show for fans at Reading festival, 1993

As the deadline for the album's completion beckoned, the singer had embarked on a lost weekend. A lost weekend that lasted for two weeks, during which he started smoking crack and by doing so, created a vicious circle for himself. He'd find himself unable to sing because he'd smoked too much crack, so he'd get depressed, smoke more crack, damage his throat, get depressed again . . . and so on.

Unfortunately, right at the height of this lost weekend, Evan was scheduled to meet the UK music press.

When the critics flew out to meet him in August 1993, they found that – far from laying down vocal tracks for the album – Evan couldn't even speak! Or so the singer claimed.

'I partied too much for too long in LA,' he wrote in a note to the *NME*'s John Mulvey, 'and it fucked up my voice.

'I'm doing OK,' he added, non-verbally. 'This not talking is just infuriating a little. My voice works, but it is in danger of getting really fucked up and I need to sing extra good before I finish the record. My vocal chords are all red and swollen.'

The problem was that Evan both loves and hates LA, simultaneously. It attracts him for the way it keeps the myth of rock 'n' roll alive, but repulses him because of its shallowness, its insincerity. The only way to cope is by throwing yourself wholeheartedly into the downward spiral of continual partying, and that's precisely what the singer did.

'Crack is a perfect metaphor for Los Angeles,' he wrote to Mulvey. 'It's instant gratification, but at a certain point your system also says "NO!" The city is full of pitfalls and crack is one of them.'

'Crack's weird,' he told *Q* magazine. 'It's a perverse thrill; to start smoking crack as a singer is really stupid. The humour in it was really there for me. The ritual is fun, but really,

Photo for 'Come On Feel The Lemonheads' cover

drugs make your life worse in the end. You don't have your normal glee left at all; you just have this very reliable, unnatural high. And some crack has talcum powder in it that can kill you instantly.

'I've always done dumb things on purpose,' he continued. 'I was always the guy who'd dive into the trashcan for no reason. Having done crack now, though, I'm not sure it's all it's cracked up to be. It's like (puff, puff) and then you get a 10, maybe 12 minute high. The ritual is what I found fun . . .'

Evan then went on to describe in minute detail what smoking crack was like. He was later to regret being so candid about his drug use, especially when it quickly became the only subject any of his interviewers wanted to ask him about.

'The whole fuckin' stupid drug thing that came up, that all started because the *NME* came all the way from London to talk to me in LA and I wasn't allowed to talk, so I felt like I owed them an explanation,' he explained to *Select* the next month. 'But the whole thing is getting a little bit tiresome, really.'

'It was a stupid fuck-up,' he told *Rolling Stone*. 'A joke that didn't translate.'

David feels Evan turned to crack simply because he was depressed.

'After you've been touring for a year, you begin to feel your band members are your only friends,' the drummer explains. 'What happened, I think, was that after Nic and I had gone, Evan felt pretty lonely. So he started hanging out with a crowd who were kind of cool, cos they were junkies – and they became his friends all of a sudden, his professional friends. For the 10 minutes you're on it, crack makes you feel the person you're with is your best friend in the world.

'Also, there was all that stuff going down with people telling us we were great. I was feeling frustrated and intolerant by the time I left – and he had to stick around after that. He was the one who really had to face it. Maybe he took crack as a passive/aggressive reaction against that. Maybe he wanted people to stop telling him he was great. Maybe he wanted someone to yell at him occasionally. Evan knew there were deadlines for the record and

David Ryan, Amsterdam, 1993

he also knew that smoking crack was the most self-destructive thing he could do – physically, and for his career. That he'd ruin his voice.

'The ironic thing was that he didn't actually smoke all that much, but the day he lost his voice was when he did all the press.'

Evan Dando, Glastonbury, 1993

When it comes down to it, Evan's just a boy who can't say no. But that doesn't make him a crackhead.

Period.

DRESS AND PIGTAILS?

Earlier that year, Evan had already courted controversy by his behaviour at a couple of festivals in Britain.

At Reading, in August, he took to the stage wearing a flower-printed dress and pigtails – producing the singer's favourite Lemonheads review ever: 'It makes serious music journalism futile.' The outfit came from a girl he knew in LA called Estelle. When, almost predictably, Juliana appeared for an encore of 'It's About Time', he rewarded her loyalty by planting a big lascivious kiss on her lips.

Earlier in the day, just after a truncated signing session in the *Maker* tent, he caused a near-riot by wandering out for a photo shoot into a long line of fans still patiently waiting for his autograph. It was only through the diligent actions of his just-appointed minder (your humble writer), he escaped unscathed.

A month before, at Glastonbury festival, Evan caused even more trouble by almost not turning up at all. The *Maker*'s on-the-spot roaming reporter, Peter Paphides, takes up the story:

'. . . meanwhile, backstage, there are lots of worried-looking people running around with walkie talkies.

'The Lemonheads, it appears, haven't arrived and yet they're due on in half-an-hour. Just as a replacement act is announced, a battered estate car trundles into the backstage area. In it, a bemused Evan Dando waves back as I catch his attention.

' "Weeeyy!! Evan! Why are you so late?" I shout.

' "I was thrown off the airplane," shrugs the compliant Lemonhead. "I had to wait for another. I took a Polaroid picture of a stewardess, and I wrote a little 'Hello' on it and gave it to her. She got real upset about that. And then she called one of her superiors over, and they gave me a speaking-to. At which point, I asked the superior guy what his mother's maiden name was. And they took me off the plane!"

Catapulted into the major league, The Lemonheads live has become a bigger event than ever

"What was the problem?"

' "I was a little drunk, I must admit," grins a slightly sheepish Evan. "Technically, it's sexual harassment, so I guess that's why they threw me off. And I did say the word 'tosser' once. But only because I thought she wasn't English and she wouldn't understand what it meant. You'll be glad to know I'm sober now." . . . '

Later that evening, Evan could be found performing one of his favourite chat-up tricks: playing solo to a bunch of wide-eyed girls sitting round a campfire. Onstage, Nic Dalton vaulted 10 feet off the stage, straight into the photographer's pit, and then into the crowd.

And they claim rock 'n' roll is dead!

BAND OF DREAMS

In December 1993, The Lemonheads embarked on a week-long mini-tour of America with Hole to help promote 'Come On Feel The Lemonheads'.

By this point, it was apparent that Evan had become the darling of the Hollywood brat-pack film cognoscenti. At the band's show in

LA, Drew Barrymore and Rosanna Arquette were spotted swanning around backstage, among others.

(Evan even has a cameo appearance in the forthcoming Winona Ryder picture, *Reality Bites*.)

Juliana and Evan had a major bust-up after he refused to let her sing onstage with the band, so she went down to his dressing room later, to present him with a cockroach wrapped in silver foil!

In a review of the show, I wrote: 'Tonight, The Lemonheads are probably no better and no worse than before – yet, because I'm familiar with the songs, they sound like the most ravished, ravenous band of my dreams. "Big Gay Heart", where Evan breaks down halfway through and the crowd half-moan, half-croon the chorus back at him, is particularly luminous . . . '

Afterwards, we all tried to dodge the ubiquitous drug-dealers hanging backstage, and discussed the embarrassment of having girls screaming at you wherever you go.

As if I should be so lucky!

THE VOICE

Yet despite all the press and attendant media hype, as well as a Top 10 entry in the UK for the album, 'Come On Feel The Lemonheads' hasn't cracked the US market the way most people expected it to (it eventually peaked at Number 56 on Billboard).

Reading festival, 1993

Despite Evan's increasingly public persona – he was named in an end-of-year poll in *People* magazine as one of the world's 50 Dishiest People – perhaps The Lemonheads' friendly, poppy sound is *too* friendly and poppy for its own good. This, after all, is a time when the much-harsher, much more inaccessible and moodier Seattle trio of Soundgarden, Pearl Jam and Nirvana are debuting on Billboard at Number One.

Or perhaps it's simply because the band haven't 'worked' the album hard enough.

'It didn't surprise me that much that "Come On" didn't take off in the US,' says Nic. 'We only toured there for a total of five weeks, and over in America you have to "tour the album". I was a little surprised, however, because it's a great record. Maybe boys are put off from buying it because The Lemonheads are meant to be a band their sister likes. That's not Evan's fault. He'll go along with the flow in interviews as far as being perceived as an airhead, because he doesn't care. When you have to do a million interviews a day, you might as well take the easy route offered to you. People are going to write what they're going to write, anyway.

'Evan's not like that at all, not the Evan I know. I wouldn't hang around someone if they were really like that. He's not an airhead at all. He's a Pisces, so he might seem like his head is in a cloud. But he talks, he has conversations, he does all the normal social things people do – reads, watches television and eats good food. He likes to flirt, but everyone flirts. He's not a slut, though. He doesn't sleep around at all. So he likes to kiss girls – don't we all!

'No one's normal in a band,' the bassist continues, 'but Evan is as normal as the next person. When I'm away from all this in Australia, it seems like another world. Sometimes, it's pretty bizarre. I tend to forget what a funny little phenomenon it is I'm part of.'

So what would you say is The Lemonheads' strongest asset?

'Evan's voice,' replies Nic Dalton firmly. 'He has a great voice.'

The Lemonheads – Nic, Evan, David, 1994